July - 22 . 07

"Tom Harken is a living testament to the literacy cause,
and I know [his] inspirational story will help many people."
—Barbara Bush
Former First Lady, Literacy Advocate

The Real
Tom Harken

To: Austin
" Enjoy "

Tom Harken
ii

More praise for Tom and Melba Harken and
The Millionaire's Secret

"Tom Harken's story is a perfect example of the power of the human spirit to overcome adversity."

—General Colin L. Powell, USA (Ret.)
Former Chairman, Joint Chiefs of Staff

". . . inspires and instructs us all. *The Millionaire's Secret* is the story of his and Miss Melba's love for and faith in each other and our country."

—Clarence Thomas
Justice, United States Supreme Court

"This book is one of the most honest, inspiring, and moving stories ever lived. Tom and Miss Melba have inspired me to give more and love more, and I know they will do the same for you."

—Wally Amos
Founder, Famous Amos and Uncle Noname

"Your story is compelling, dynamic, absorbing, and inspiring."

—Walter Anderson
Editor, *Parade* magazine

"I truly believe Tom Harken and Miss Melba are called by God to help many in this way, and my prayer is that *The Millionaire's Secret* will advance your unique 'ministry of literacy.'"

—Rev. Jerry Falwell
Founder and Chancellor, Liberty University

"Tom Harken is indeed a living Horatio Alger story who has triumphed over adversity and touched the lives of so many with his hopeful message."

—George L. Argyros
Chairman and CEO, Arnel & Affiliates

"Tom has proved again that the American dream is a reality waiting to happen if you work at it and make it happen."
—W. W. "Foots" Clements
Chairman Emeritus, Dr Pepper Company

"I am glad Tom and Miss Melba have decided to share their amazing life story in this book to encourage, inspire, and teach so many through their beautiful and triumphant relationship."
—S. Truett Cathy
Founder and Chairman, Chick-fil-A, Inc.

"Tom and Melba Harken's story is matched only by the enthusiasm with which Tom shares it . . . I encourage you to read this vital book."

—Ruth Colvin
Founder, Literacy Volunteers of America

"Tom and Melba Harken's story will stir your soul and enrich your life, and you will find yourself wanting to share it with your friends."

—Robert H. Dedman
Founder and Chairman, ClubCorp International

"Tom Harken is one of the most inspirational Americans of our day . . . With Tom and Miss Melba, the difficult gets done immediately and the impossible takes only a little longer."
—Terry M. Giles
President, Giles Enterprises

"Tom Harken is pied piper to the younger generation as they follow him into the world of readers. *The Millionaire's Secret* shows why."

—Dr. John Silber
Chancellor, Boston University
Chairman, Massachusetts Board of Education

"*The Millionaire's Secret* is rife with compassion, ambition, determination, perseverance, courage, and human understanding. It is a must read! You will walk away all fired up to pursue your dreams and do your best."

—Dr. Jack Gill
Silicon Valley Technologist, Entrepreneur,
and Venture Capitalist

"If anyone in the world ever pulled himself up by his own bootstraps, it is Tom Harken. And he did it with integrity, grace, faith, and Miss Melba. Tom is a joyous, giving friend, articulate and thoughtful, as the reader will learn."

—Peter J. Jannetta, M.D.
Chairman, Neurological Surgery, University of Pittsburgh
School of Medicine

"What can you say about Tom and Melba Harken other than the fact they are two unique people who combined their wonderful spirits and formed a phenomenon that can be called a marriage, a partnership, or a two-ring circus headlined by a gregarious, loving 'teddy bear' and backed by a caring, thoughtful, ever-present Miss Melba."

—James R. "Jim Bob" Moffett
Chairman and CEO, Freeport McMoRan
Copper & Gold Inc.

"Tom Harken's challenge to overcome illiteracy and rise to success makes his story unique in all of America."

—Richard L. Knowlton
Chairman Emeritus, Hormel Co.,
Chairman, The Hormel Foundation

"Tom Harken is an exceptional example of America at its finest . . . With the help and encouragement of Miss Melba, Tom has demonstrated that dreams can indeed be reality."

—Joseph Neubauer
Chairman and CEO, Aramark Corporation

"Tom Harken, with the strong support of Miss Melba, has turned his adversity of illiteracy into an articulate example of hope for millions of Americans."

—John V. Roach
CEO and Chairman, Tandy Corporation

"We watched tears in our children's eyes as you shared your story with them. You are both so real, so human, and so loving."

—John Rollins
Chairman and CEO, Rollins Truck Leasing Corporation

"Tom and Miss Melba exemplify the old saying 'Behind every good man is a great lady' . . . Only in America could someone like Tom Harken make it to the top without being able to read."

—Charles "Red" Scott
CEO, The Executive Committee of Florida

"Thank you so much for sharing your compelling story with the millions of adults in this country who lack literacy skills. You are truly a hero and an inspiration! I know that others will find the courage to seek help because of you."

—Marsha L. Tait
President, Literacy Volunteers of America

"Tom Harken's story of adversity in overcoming illiteracy with Miss Melba's help is awesome. Sharing his triumph and giving hope to others to achieve as much is equally outstanding."

—Dr. Arthur E. Turner
Founder, Northwood University,
Chairman, Northwood Institute

"Reading about Tom Harken's life will make you cry and smile all at the same time. Tom's story is 100 percent all-American. With the love of his family and the protection of his Maker, nothing was impossible."

—Jack H. Brown
Chairman, President, and CEO, Stater Bros. Markets

"Tom, I see they finally got you out of the kitchen. Wish I could be there to lead the applause."

—Bob Hope
Entertainer
(at Horatio Alger Award ceremonies,
Washington, D.C., 1992)

THE Millionaire's Secret

Tom Harken
with Don Jacobs

THOMAS NELSON PUBLISHERS
Nashville

Published in Nashville, Tennessee, by Thomas Nelson, Inc., Publishers.

Library of Congress Cataloging-in-Publication Data

Harken, Tom.
    The millionaire's secret : Tom Harken, with Don Jacobs.
      p.   cm.
    ISBN 0-7852-7727-7
    1. Harken, Tom.   2. Restaurateurs—United States—Biography. I. Jacobs, Don. II. Title.
    TX910.5.H33A3 1998
    647.95'092—dc21
    [B]   98-34229
                                         CIP

Printed in the United States of America.

2 3 4 5 6 QW 07 06 05

To Miss Melba
This is my love letter to you.

Contents

Foreword

✦·What you are about to read is the story of a man worth knowing and a life worth emulating. I first met Tom Harken in April 1994, when I had the honor of being a recipient of the Horatio Alger Award. Tom—who was much more deserving than I—had received it in 1992 and was attending the annual award ceremony, where such recipients as Colin Powell, Maya Angelou, and Bob Hope have customarily gathered.

I took an instant liking to this cheerful, down-to-earth, self-made restaurant executive who, like all Horatio Alger winners, had overcome adversity to achieve success. In fact, I was so impressed with his outgoing personality and admirable accomplishments that I promptly assigned a reporter to write a cover story about him for *Parade* magazine and its eighty million readers. I'm also glad to say that I was among those who encouraged him to write this book, in which he recounts his remarkable battle to overcome the devastating effects of illness and years of illiteracy.

It requires courage for a man—especially a successful man—to stand up and acknowledge publicly that he learned to read at such a late age and had gotten through life utilizing such tricks as always ordering burgers in restaurants because he couldn't decipher a printed menu. Tom Harken is a proud man, but he did that. And while he recognizes that he probably never could have learned to read without the loving help of his devoted wife, whom he affectionately calls "Miss Melba"—and who shares the pages of this book with him—it also was a task requiring plenty of guts and determination on his part.

This is about how self-reliance and self-determination can conquer inner fears and outward challenges. It's a human and heartening story, and I hope you find it as moving—and, yes, as inspiring—as I do. And I promise that, before you put it down, you'll discover that Tom Harken is a man who cannot only read but also write.

—Walter Anderson
Editor of *Parade* magazine,
Member of the National
Commission on Libraries and
Information Science, Advisory
Board Member of Literacy
Volunteers of America and the
National Center for Family
Literacy

Preface

᛭Melba Janiece Curtis was the eighth of ten children, born on a dust-bowl farm in southwestern Oklahoma toward the end of the depression. Her parents were uneducated but hardworking people of high moral standards, and they expected their children to develop those characteristics. Above all, they wanted all of them to finish high school, then go out and find good jobs so life would be better for them. They had no indoor plumbing, and young Melba grew up feeding chickens and pigs and picking cotton. Every once in a while, after their chores she and her sister would go up to their playhouse—a cave they had discovered in the side of a mountain bordering the family property. It was a secret spot about a hundred yards from the drive leading to the house, and they could see all that went on down at the farm.

It was an era in which neighbors helped neighbors. When you got your crops in, you went and helped others get theirs harvested. It was tough work, but as far as Melba was concerned it wasn't a tough life, and it shaped her character. That's just the way it was, and Melba set the same uncompromising standards for herself at school as she had in the fields at home. By the time she graduated from high school at seventeen, Melba was captain of the all-star basketball team, the straight-A valedictorian of her class—and a straight-A human being.

But that wasn't what impressed me when we were first introduced by a mutual friend who thought we were made for each other. I was a smart-alecky twenty-year-old kid with a big mouth and a chip on my shoulder, and all I saw at first was a great-looking, tall blonde. "Wow," I said to myself, turning on the boyish charm. Well, I set out to impress the heck out of this "country girl," figuring she would be easily dazzled. Wrong! I stupidly talked too much, too fast, and made little, if any, sense. She was pleasant and polite for a while, but I soon sensed a coolness in her attitude. The evening was definitely not a success, but I did drive her home that night. I figured I pretty much ruined any chances I may have had with her, so it was a couple of weeks before I got up the nerve to call her and ask her out. I couldn't believe it, but she actually agreed to a date. The second meeting would prove to be much more successful—I managed to calm down, relax a bit, and be myself—and we began what was to become a very long and wonderful life together.

That was forty years ago. I don't know what she saw in me, but there must have been something. It would have been charitable to call me rough around the edges at that point in my life. I was immature and irresponsible, self-indulgent and self-destructive—even after we got married. A year or so later, we started having children, and like most people we came close to breaking up several times. But it had to be God who brought us together and kept us together. Melba stuck through it all, loving to me even when I wasn't to her, tough when she had to be, reaffirming my faith in myself, and inspiring me to do the best I could do. Finally, I began to grow up, and into the kind of man I never thought I was capable of becoming—but she says she always knew I had it in me.

And all because of her. From humble beginnings and tragic reverses that only deep love and deeper faith could possibly survive, we have endured and triumphed together. With her at my side, we've managed to make all our dreams come true. Dreams that would have died on the vine without her. There's no doubt in my mind that without Miss Melba, as I've always affectionately called her, I wouldn't even be here. Nor would we have our two fantastic sons, two beautiful daughters-in-law, or our three wonderful grandchildren. I wouldn't want to be here without her. In words I never thought I'd use, we're simply "soul mates." And will be until the day we die.

I just read this to her, and we shed a few tears together. But then, as usual, she had the last word: "Not even then, honey. You're stuck with me forever."

Thank God.

—Tom Harken

Acknowledgments

❧Wow! The book is called *The Millionaire's Secret,* but it's no secret that it took many people to make it happen. Since 1992 alone we have welcomed hundreds of new friends and associates into our lives, and I will strive not to omit a single deserving name. I am personally thanking each individual who had a part in producing our story, and I acknowledge them here for all the world to see.

First, I want to thank those who demonstrated the perseverance, found the patience, and withstood the pressure to see this project through from beginning to end—Miss Melba, of course, along with Victor Gonzalez, my friend and company president, and Sara Lake, our vice president and special assistant. When my liaison officer and I failed, Sara's feminine approach was very instrumental in convincing Miss Melba—at a time when there was some reluctance concerning the writing of the book—to go ahead with it. From Victor to our office manager, Luthena Highfill, to our entire office staff, all have had to endure a great deal of added frustration because of this book. Along with helping to run our busy corporate offices, they have dealt with everything from having VIP visitors underfoot to taking telephone calls from all over the world pertaining to speech and interview requests.

Without hesitation I want to add that if not for another individual, the book would not have been written; I speak of my liaison officer, Don Jacobs. He often says if I ever learn to spell *liaison* he won't have a job. Don't worry about it, pal. Don has traveled with me on hundreds of trips to make speeches, and on one occasion when I was too sick to get out bed, he even pinch-hit for me. The bad thing about that is, they didn't ask me to come back, they asked *him*. Hmm. Thank you, Don, again and again.

On to Walter Anderson, who wrote the foreword, and S. Truett Cathy, both of whom planted the seeds of thought at different times. Without their encouragement, no doubt this book wouldn't exist. Thanks to Dr. Robert H. Schuller for his thoughtful introduction to the book. Dr. Schuller also introduced us to that lady who would become my literary agent, which, by the way, is a relatively new word in my vocabulary. Lois de la Haba doesn't fit the stereotype because this absolutely, wonderfully amazing New York lady has a heart as big as Texas—and what a negotiator she is. Holy guacamole!

Writer Norm Rohrer was instrumental in the selection of a portion of our book's title. Financial consultants Dave Thomas and Tommy Polk got the ball rolling by recommending me for nomination to the Horatio Alger Association—and at the time they didn't even know our secret: my illiteracy.

Many thanks and much appreciation go to Thomas Nelson, Inc., for the faith they took in us, and in the book, by taking on publication of it. The professionalism demonstrated by this revered company, now celebrating an unprecedented two-hundredth anniversary, is outstanding. Such excellence always starts with the leader at the top, and that would be one Mr. Sam Moore, who became an instant friend the moment we met. The editorial talents of Janet Thoma and her capable assistant, Todd Ross, are to be commended, along with Brenda White, vice president of production in the Thomas Nelson Book Division. Also Sharon Gilbert, head of author relations, and Blythe McIntosh, publicity manager.

Special thanks to all my Horatio Alger Association friends, and my compliments to those involved in the battle against illiteracy the world over.

To the dear friends who endorsed this book and otherwise commented on our love for literacy, I wish to pay hearty thanks. These include Wally Amos, Walter Anderson, George L. Argyros, Jack Brown, Barbara Bush, S. Truett Cathy, W. W. "Foots" Clements, Ruth Colvin, Robert H. Dedman, the Rev. Jerry Falwell, Terry M. Giles, Dr. Jack Gill, Mark Victor Hansen, Bob Hope, H. Wayne Huizenga, Dr. Peter J. Jannetta, Dr. Henry A. Kissinger, Richard L. Knowlton, Ed McMahon, James R. "Jim Bob" Moffett, Joseph Neubauer, Dr. Jean Nidetch, Ruth Stafford Peale, General Colin L. Powell, Dr. John V. Roach, John Rollins Sr., Charles "Red" Scott, John Silber, Dr. Robert B. Sloan Jr., Marsha L. Tait, Justice Clarence Thomas, and Dr. Arthur E. Turner.

I would be remiss if I didn't acknowledge the patience of our sons, Tommy and Mark; along with daughters-in-law Debra and Staci; and especially our dear grandchildren, Trace, McKenzie, and Terran (in order of age). They never seem to have enough time with their "Poppee," and that is one area I plan to start improving on; trust me, kids.

I would also like to acknowledge Kathryn and Fred Harken, my mom and dad. I miss them terribly. Also, credit goes to early and longtime mentors and friends Marie Southern and her late husband, Casey, and the late Ben and Julie Rogers. To those whose names I may have inadvertently omitted, please forgive. Our next book is in the works.

Introduction

❧I know of no one who has more dramatically tapped the secrets of success than Tom Harken of Beaumont, Texas. It was my great honor to introduce to the global audience of *The Hour of Power* my fellow member in the Horatio Alger Association. The first qualification for members in the association is that they had to begin with virtually nothing and, believe me, Tom certainly qualifies as that type of individual.

At a very young age Tom was busy literally fighting for his life and missed a lot of school. When he returned to school he was "a very big kid at a very little desk." The teacher and fellow pupils made fun of him because he couldn't read or write. In shame and frustration, Tom finally quit school to face the world as an illiterate.

This book records Tom's struggles, which led eventually to the pinnacle of success. Today, in addition to championing the cause of literacy, Tom directs a multimillion-dollar business providing excellent career opportunities for his associates and pleasurable experiences for all who dine in his restaurants.

The price he paid to get there was heavy. The best part is that his secrets will work for you too.

—Dr. Robert H. Schuller
Founder and Senior Pastor
Crystal Cathedral Ministries
Garden Grove, California

Prologue

❧ Wow! I wrote a book!

It wasn't that long ago I couldn't even *read* a book. God has blessed me in many ways in my sixty-one years on this earth. I've become a millionaire and something of a success in the eyes of the world. I've met—and stood in awe of—hundreds of famous people and brought many of them to my home in southeast Texas. I've been honored and humbled by being presented the Horatio Alger Award in 1992.

I've known pain too. I was ill for years and spent one day short of a year in an iron lung, a victim of polio as a kid. Quarantined to a single room in my home for another long period, I also had tuberculosis; doctors feared I might still be contagious.

Those illnesses changed my life, and I relate this now to the best of my ability and recollection. Some of the details are vague and cloudy—much of it I *wanted* to forget, and some of it I just can't remember—such as the exact years things happened and how old I was at the time. I only wish my parents were here to fill in the blanks, but this is my story. I don't bear the physical scars as do many victims of those childhood diseases. My scars are mental ones. Because I lost so much time in school, I never learned to read. I am an elementary school dropout.

I kept my illiteracy and those scars hidden for much of my life. It was only when I realized that I would receive the Horatio Alger Award with such luminaries as Henry Kissinger, Maya Angelou, Justice Clarence Thomas, and six other remarkable and noteworthy individuals that I realized we (my wife, Melba, and I were the only two who knew my secret) had to tell my story. The whole story.

That's what this book is all about. It's the story of a kid who grew up in Michigan but never learned to read. It's the story of a young man who, by the grace of God, met a woman who helped him overcome that handicap and eventually conquer his illiteracy. It's the story of how that man and that woman made successes of three different businesses and who today run a chain of restaurants in southeast Texas and Louisiana, providing excellent jobs and an above-average quality of life for hundreds of people.

This is the story of a person who had some bad breaks along the way but who worked hard and persevered until good things began to happen.

Only in America could this story have come true, and based on the numbers I see heading for our shores, I believe that only in America can your dreams come true. There are many things to love about this country, and one of them is opportunity.

I also love good, positive stories. I hope this book will give you a lift. It's easy to find bad news anywhere you turn. I think Americans once again need to stand up and say, "Let's have some good news for a change."

The Millionaire's Secret is my good news story.

My father always said, "Tommy, there are givers and there are takers. The takers, they eat real good. But the givers, they sleep a lot better. Now, it's your choice which direction you go."

I'm not sure why, but I have chosen to be a giver. Maybe it's my means of honoring the memory of my late father in the only way I know how, and glorifying God for the same reason.

I can't see God, but I can feel His presence. You can, too, and it is one of the most exhilarating and inspiring feelings granted to us mortals. When we give from the heart, helping someone in need and expecting nothing in return, we truly are touching the hand of God.

You may be faced with the same choice I confronted as a blundering, illiterate, and immature young man. If I can make sense out of a senseless life, you can, too, or help someone else to do it. If I can encourage illiterates to seek help and others to become tutors—and encourage you to do the same—my mission is well on the way to being accomplished. But we need tens of thousands more volunteers; the number of illiterates is far greater than we previously realized.

Be a giver.

—Tom Harken

1

"Only in America"

My life changed at the Horatio Alger Awards
when I finally told the world my secret.

❖❖❖❖❖❖❖❖❖❖❖❖❖❖❖❖❖❖❖❖❖❖❖❖

❧ *This can't be happening. Not to a little, short, fat guy who sells tacos for a living in Texas.* These were my thoughts in Washington, D.C., on the evening of May 1, 1992, far from home and feeling a little bit guilty because I wasn't back in Beaumont greeting and seating diners in one of my Mexican restaurants. That's where I'm most comfortable. Instead, there I was, along with a Who's Who of "distinguished Americans" who had been selected to receive the prestigious Horatio Alger Award. It is presented each year to a group of men and women who have overcome adversity and pulled themselves up by their own bootstraps in the classic tradition of American success stories and the free enterprise system. It's true that I overcame adversity and pulled myself up, with a lot of help. But distinguished? I don't know about that.

While Miss Melba and I stood in a foyer at the Grand Hyatt Hotel's Independence Ballroom waiting for the hundreds of Horatio Alger Association members and guests to be seated and the ceremonies to begin, I glanced nervously around at my fellow recipients. Over there was Dick Knowlton, head of the Hormel Company. He looked cool as a cucumber, and I was standing there feeling like a side of bacon. The great poet laureate and professor, Maya Angelou, was there, tall, regal, and serene. I knew her acceptance speech would be pure poetry, and I could already feel myself getting mush-mouthed.

Me and my fellow award winners former Secretary of State Henry Kissinger and Blockbuster Chairman Wayne Huizenga at the 1992 Horatio Alger Awards ceremony

Miss Melba and I were nervous, all right. She hadn't had a good night's sleep in days, and for me it was probably more like weeks. I was worked up to a fever pitch, and there was no telling what I might say or do at any given moment. Miss Melba just kept saying silent prayers.

Looking accustomed to accepting such awards were John Silber, then president, and on his way to becoming chancellor, of Boston University, and the dignified and friendly James Rouse, who had created Faneuil Hall Marketplace in Boston and Harborplace in Baltimore. Former Secretary of Agriculture John Block stood by quietly, alongside Jack Brown, head man at Stater Bros. Markets. He looked about as nervous as I felt. And even in repose, Supreme Court Associate Justice Clarence Thomas seemed to have a thousand things on his mind, but he had a ready smile.

Melba and I have become good friends with
Justice Clarence Thomas.

I'd been to ultra-formal, black-tie affairs before, and owned a couple of tuxes to prove it, but at this one I was in awe, wondering what in the world I was doing in this kind of company— and they had to be wondering the same thing about me. Especially when I began making conversation with two men who were standing nearby. Melba had warned me not to say anything I shouldn't, because as she puts it, I never seem to know what I'm going to say until I hear it. It's a good thing she was already seated inside when I turned to fellow award winners former Secretary of State Henry Kissinger and Blockbuster Video Chairman Wayne Huizenga and heard myself saying, "Well, I don't know how I got here, but if it has anything to do with looks, they must have called me first. I'm not much, but I'm better looking than *both* of you." I wanted to sink into the carpeting, but after an awkward moment of silence, Kissinger recognized my intended humor and threw in a little of his own dry wit simply by smiling in my direction as if comparing me to a rotunda. We all laughed. The ice was broken.

As the strains of the Horatio Alger theme song, "Only in America," signaled us to file through the audience to our tables, we were applauded by a roomful of a thousand or so guests that included internationally renowned award recipients from earlier years: General Colin Powell, then chairman of the Joint Chiefs of Staff; Mary Kay Cosmetics founder Mary Kay Ash; Weight Watchers founder Jean Nidetch; the Reverend Robert Schuller; world-famous brain surgeon Dr. Peter Jannetta; test pilot General Chuck Yeager; and beloved author and television personality Art Linkletter.

Trying not to let it show, I gazed around in awe at such famous people as trucking magnate John Rollins, whose subdued yet powerful demeanor just absolutely scared the popcorn out of me; mining legend Jim Bob Moffett; timber baron Harry Merlo; and S. Truett Cathy, Robert Dedman, Thomas Haggai, Don Keough, Venita VanCaspel—all these greats, and many more. As I sat down between my wife and another legend, W. W. Clements, who would present my award, I looked around at the sea of faces throughout the room, overcome with a sense of unreality, and my throat began to tighten.

I saw the tables we had reserved, trying to spot those who

had made the trip with us, but although huge in area, the room was jam-packed with people. Now and then, I'd spot our tall sons introducing themselves to various ones, shaking hands and chatting, and then I'd get a glimpse of Debra and Staci, our daughters-in-law, and this friend or that. The room vibrated with excitement, and everywhere we looked, women were in gowns costing more than we'd paid for our first house. Beside Melba, Virginia Clements was a picture of calmness, having experienced all this so many times, while it definitely was our first.

Sensing the anxiety that was overwhelming me, Melba reached out to squeeze my hand and calm me with a smile. At that moment, I couldn't even speak—but it was as if she had her arms around me, and all the struggles, all the triumphs we'd shared for all the years that took us to this destination, washed over me in a wave of memory.

2

Ready to Take on the World

Me and my brother hard at play
Even at age four, I had a singular determination.

❖❖❖❖❖❖❖❖❖❖❖❖❖❖❖❖❖❖❖❖❖❖❖❖❖❖❖❖

☙When I was born in Mt. Pleasant, Michigan, on the morning of February 10, 1937, no one was more surprised than my parents were. I wasn't due for another three weeks, but I guess I couldn't be bothered to wait around taking it easy when there was a life waiting to be lived. As far as I was concerned, it was time to get going, and that's all there was to it. A 1941 photo captured me at the age of four working hard at *playing* in a backyard mud puddle in the Land of Lakes. The expression on the young face reveals an impatience beyond my years, a fed-upness with childhood, an urgency to reach maturity and get on with it. I remember having that sense of urgency even then.

If it had been up to me, I would have gotten up, tracked mud right through the house, and walked out the front door, ready to take on the world.

That's almost what I did. From the time I was old enough to toddle, I hit the ground running every morning, and my mother, Kathryn, practically had to strap me back in bed at night. Before I was six, I was welcome in the kitchen of every house on the block and knew every kid and canine in the neighborhood. My older brother had his friends, and I had mine. We were a typical family, even when my adopted sister came along, and much later when another sister was born—sharing like all children the usual generational distances and familial togetherness, from chilly differences to warm dinners.

We Harken children enjoyed our own circles of friends and recreational interests. I loved marbles and Chinese checkers, and when it came to tricks with a yo-yo, I could make one talk and the other kids marvel. Playing ball was another of my passions. I loved it all—baseball, basketball, football, any kind of ball. But I just couldn't seem to get anything off the ground when it came to the usual classroom studies. Today, they would have called me an underachiever, but even then I was painfully aware of being slower than the rest of the class. Learning disabilities were virtually unheard of in those days, and children were either considered smart or dumb, fast or slow. Doodling and daydreaming, I had a tendency to sit at my desk and gaze out the window while the other kids learned their ABCs. Sometimes they even called me stupid. Believe me, that wasn't conducive to learning.

By this time, we were living in Lakeview, a picturesque community in central Michigan with tree-shaded homes and friendly family businesses like the one owned by my father, Fred Harken. Being in the grocery business, he'd had an opportunity to better himself in Lakeview, which was closer to my mother's hometown of Big Rapids. Later, when television's *Leave It to*

Beaver went on the air, it must have been modeled after our street. Not only did Lakeview leave its doors unlocked, most places had signs saying, "Open, come in."

My parents, Fred and Kathryn Harken

Dad was a solid worker of hardy German stock, a man respected for his integrity and beloved for his openhearted spirit. Fred Harken was also the kind of guy who'd listen to everybody's story, get involved in community affairs, and go the extra mile to help people. He had regular charge accounts for farmers and factory workers who didn't have the cash to pay for their purchases at the store; many of them never did. And if the family across the street was having a tough time getting by, he would give them a few dollars to tide them over. Dad preferred to let my mother be the tough one in the family, and she often chided him for letting people take advantage of his generosity.

He'd just smile and go on about his business of making sure a patent medicine reached a penniless old-timer, or a meaty soup bone found its way to the home of someone with hungry kids and a month's worth of overdue grocery bills. My mother would caution him, "Just don't get carried away," but she really loved that generous heart of his, and she did her share too—looking in on sick neighbors and cooking hot meals for the needy.

As different as they were from each other, the two of them were connected by a close bond. They had their interests, and they allowed us to have ours. At the time I wondered if there was enough affection to go around, but later I would thank them for the independent attitude they fostered in me. They would listen to our questions and comments around the supper table, but I always had the feeling they might just as soon be talking to each other. And every night after the evening meal, they would sit and play pinochle or gin rummy, no matter what was going on around them. We'd go to bed, and they'd still be playing cards. That's just the way it was in those days. No television.

But they didn't ignore us—far from it. Mom was vivacious and happy, and she would involve us kids in whatever she had going at any given time. She loved practical jokes. At age four or so, I loved it when she would tickle me into gales of laughter, or give me a warm comforting hug after some mishap or other, but most of the attention I got from Mom was in the form of pranks and practical jokes. She'd shout, "Boo!" when she came up behind me while I was listening to *The Shadow* or *Inner Sanctum* on the radio. And on April Fools' Day, she was likely to serve me a baloney sandwich with a sheet of paper hidden inside. Because of her, I grew up with a wide streak of playfulness myself. But I never seemed to get enough of what we need most deeply from a mother: simple nurturing and affection.

I knew she loved me, and in his own way, so did Dad, but at

home and at work, he was a no-nonsense kind of guy, always busy and preoccupied, always thinking of business. And when he wasn't working, he was doing favors for others—but seldom for his own kids. He never seemed to have time for *me* when I was a little boy, and on some level I think I resented that. But I admired him very much, because there were no flaws in his character. Right and wrong to him were black-and-white: "This is the way it is, and that's that." He was a deeply religious man, and he did his best to pass along his faith to the kids, taking us to church every Sunday without fail. My mother observed her faith more privately and seldom went with us to church, but she would send us off with a smile, saying, "You go ahead, and I'll have dinner on the stove when you get home." Her delicious Sunday dinners were always something to think about while we were nodding off in the pew.

Early on, Dad would let me hang around the grocery after school and on weekends. This was in the early days before grocery carts, invented in the '30s, rolled into Lakeview. It's a good thing, too, since I probably would have used them for joyriding. But like a playful puppy, I managed to get into things anyway, spilling syrup or sitting on the cereal boxes. I tried to help out by scattering the oiled sawdust he sprinkled on the wooden planking to keep the dust down in the store, but I wound up spilling more on the shelves than on the floor. He didn't seem to mind. He'd been a boy, too, and besides, he had the patience of Job. Even when I played with the long pole gripper he used to grab packages from the top shelves. When I attempted it, most of the items landed on the floor. That had to be annoying, but he never said a word about it. Dad knew I'd never listen if he told me what to do—and especially what *not* to do. Trial and error was the only way I seemed to learn anything.

I asked for a candy bar one day, and he said I'd have to wait until after lunch. Wandering out of his sight and down a store aisle a while later, I spied a package of Baker's unsweetened chocolate, normally used in cooking, and I thought, *Wow! Why did they put these big candy bars back here instead of with the rest of the candy up front?* But I helped myself to one and gobbled it down. Within a few minutes, I was headed for the back door trying to hold it down and having no luck. Not only was there no sympathy from Dad, he pretended not even to notice my sad plight. Sick as a dog, and no pity. It was a struggle to be a kid, especially since I was already into the first stages of a vicious disease and no one knew it. I missed a lot of school from the very beginning, but then there were times I felt fine and would help out around the store. I might have been full of mischief, but I wasn't lazy. Always slow in school, I couldn't read the labels on the cans and boxes, but there were usually pictures on them, and I was even faster than my brother in pulling them off the shelves when orders came in, then sacking them at the checkout. With customers following behind me, I'd carry two or three huge bags at a time to the cars parked out front, laughing and talking all the while. Tips weren't expected or given to grocery boys in those days, but I was doing it for Dad's approval anyway, not theirs.

As people walked in the door, I'd ask, "Is there something I can get for you?" I even rang up purchases on the old National cash register that loomed on the countertop. Even though I couldn't read, I was good with numbers, and I was even better with people—friendly and outgoing for my age, and I loved bullcorning the customers. They seemed to enjoy it, too, and I learned an early lesson that has stood me in good stead ever since: If you smile at people, chances are they'll smile back at you.

My brother also worked part-time in the store, and we got along the way young, competitive brothers everywhere get along. About half the time, I went around feeling small and stupid, and seemed always to be doing something I shouldn't be doing, or doing it wrong. Feeling put-upon one day, with my brother at the store working, I was poking around in his bedroom—ripe for rascality I suppose—when it occurred to me that he had more shirts than he needed and I should do something to help relieve the burden on his sagging closet poles. He was earning good money, and buying shirts was a passion of his, so I figured he wouldn't miss a few of them. I took four or five and sold them to a friend for a quarter each.

It would have been a clean caper if my friend Neil hadn't decided to go fishing one Sunday afternoon. On a family drive around the lake, my mother saw him, then did a double take and asked Dad to stop the car. She went over and asked, "Neil, where did you get that shirt?"

"Tommy sold it to me," Neil answered guiltlessly while I shrank into the upholstery of the backseat. *Uh-oh, in trouble again!*

Later, I got a job delivering the out-of-town daily. It paid five dollars a week, but I couldn't see the point of getting up so early every morning and carrying a heavy canvas bag full of newspapers all over town. Besides, I was growing weaker all the time. So I sublet the route to Neil for two dollars and fifty cents a week, thus not only earning passive income as an independent entrepreneur but generously providing employment for a friend. I was always coming up with moneymaking schemes, and, innocent though I thought them to be, I always seemed to get grounded, or at least chastised, for them.

I began to walk around the house with a chip on my shoulder, especially toward my mother, the disciplinarian. One night at dinner, Dad asked me to get a chair so that Mom could sit at the table. I refused, and he couldn't believe his ears. Apparently he figured he'd been too nice for too long, and this was the last straw. Picking up the phone, he called the constable's office and said, "I want you to come get Tommy and put him in jail. I've had it with him."

I guess I'd been somewhat spoiled and was used to getting

away with most things, so this was a real shocker for me. I looked over at Dad and gulped. He really meant it. For once, my mother thought he was being too tough on me, and they were arguing about it when the officer showed up. But Dad insisted that he take me away, and that's just what he did. I was locked up in a cell—the one they had—for an hour or so before the officer let me go home. I was an ex-con with a record. I can't say I never misbehaved again, but from that day on I sure didn't have any trouble getting my mother a chair.

Dad never blew up at me like that again, but I'm sure he wanted to after we woke up one cold winter morning to find the house virtually pulsating with heat. With a real Michigan winter howling outside, it had been my job to get up two or three times during the night to add coal to the furnace in order to keep it going. But I didn't like getting up, so at bedtime one night, I packed that furnace with enough coal to run a freight train. By morning, throbbing and glowing with built-up pressure and temperature, that thing was almost ready to blow when Dad got to it. Furious as he was, he didn't say much about it.

But Mom was loaded for bear a few weeks later when she got home one Sunday afternoon to find a mess I'd made tracking mud through the house. Time and again she had warned me about it, but this time something snapped.

"Fred," she said when Dad got home, "I want you to take Tom downstairs and spank him—right now."

Whoa! I hadn't listened to all those mystery programs for nothing. Downstairs meant the basement, where punishment could be meted out almost soundlessly as far as the outer world was concerned. Though Dad was never one to hurt a housefly, this time I experienced a sense of doom.

"But, Kathryn, it was probably just an accident."

"I don't care," she said adamantly. "You take him downstairs."

So he marched me into the basement and turned me over his knee, swatting me a couple of times on the butt. It didn't even hurt.

"Cry," he said in a low voice. "Tommy, please cry so she'll know I'm spanking you."

I pretended to cry a little, and then I walked back upstairs rubbing my eyes and trying to whimper. My mother was happy. But Dad hadn't appeared, so I went back down and there he was, sitting on the stairs and crying softly. He said, "I won't ever spank you again, Tommy. But you've got to start straightening up. Sooner or later you've got to straighten up."

Well, I took his words to heart—for a day or two. Then friend Dick Turner and I hatched the idea of putting on a circus. Dick and I were cohorts and culprits in a lot of harmless, if questionable, activities on the road to puberty. There was a double garage at his house, and upstairs was a real neat attic, and we decided this would be the perfect place for a circus. Dick and I had expensive habits—from burgers and sodas to candy bars and Cokes—and whatever we got involved in, it was for the net cash proceeds. So we charged admission for the circus, and we even had games of chance. In one of them, we filled a washtub with water then set the lid of a Mason jar faceup on the bottom. The suckers threw quarters into the water, trying to make them land in the lid. It's almost impossible to do, but we kept some quarters in the lid to make it look easy. If someone did manage to do it, he would win three quarters. Very seldom did this happen, and our pockets jingled. Dick's older brother, Bob, was one of our biggest customers, but our innocent hijinks must have taught him the error of his ways early on. He later entered the priesthood.

One afternoon sometime later, Dick and I were sitting in his garage admiring his mother's new car, a white Dodge. We had recently seen our first two-tone car and were impressed with it. Why don't we take this new car and dress it up some, we asked each other, unable to think of a single reason not to. World War II had just ended, and we were fond of military vehicles, so when we decided to repaint the fenders, we thought army green would be a tasteful shade. Since that was the only color of paint in the garage, we shut the big wooden door and went right to work with our brushes. That's right, I said brushes.

It looked pretty good, if you didn't look too closely at the bristle strokes, and if you didn't mind a few spatters where they didn't belong. We had decided to paint the fenders green and leave the rest of the car white. But we ran out of paint before finishing all four fenders. Down at the hardware store, we bought more paint, but it didn't match the first batch, so we started repainting, and spilling more as we went, until it began to look like a camouflage car. By the time we realized what we'd done, we were scared to death, and all we could think about was where to hide this monstrosity. We couldn't think where to put it, so finally we just walked off and left it there in the garage, hoping nobody would notice.

Since the car was locked in *his* garage, I figured I might not get caught, but Dick broke down under intense interrogation and gave me up in the first sixty seconds. I didn't hold it against him—if it had been my garage, I would have turned *him* in too.

But I should have thought twice about it a few months later when we were admiring my dad's new Plymouth, which was parked under a pear tree behind his store. It was lunch hour at school and very cold. Dick and I were sitting in the vehicle listening to the radio, enjoying the new car smell and feeling like big shots. "Why don't we take it for a ride?" he said casually.

"We can't do that, but Dad might let me practice shifting the gears," I told him, so we went inside and asked for a couple of candy bars and soft drinks. I also asked permission to start the car and move it a few feet. Dad was busy and had no time for our shenanigans and said no to everything.

"Just stay out of the car, Tommy," he said. "I'll teach you

how to shift it later. Isn't it time for you to get back to school anyway?"

So we went back out behind the store to the alleyway, got back into the car, and the thought hit both of us at the same time: *Let's just do it!*

Somehow we got the car started and rolling with me trying to steer and Dick operating the accelerator. Then suddenly we were moving toward the frozen lake, where ice-fishing shacks stood here and there. Applying the brakes seemed to make the car go even faster, and before we knew it, we were sliding around on the ice. Thoughts of trouble that was certain to come were distant. This was enormous fun, and we gave little thought as to whether there would be any explaining to do later. We spun around and around, this way and that, for several minutes. Being careful to avoid the shacks the farther out we went, we weren't careful enough to avoid a section of ice that was not solid.

A loud snap got our attention. The ice began giving way, and the car's rear wheels started sinking. Out we came, lucky to be alive, and scurried back to the warmth and safety of the school.

"Gosh, what are we gonna do, Tommy?" Dick asked. "This is the worst thing we've ever done."

"Maybe the car will sink and nobody will ever be able to find it," I told him. "Nobody will ever know what happened to it." We were really reaching.

Dad showed up later, and there was no point in trying to deny it. Once we were told the car was half submerged in the lake and men with tractors were enlisted to pull it out, we quit playing dumb and provided the details, hoping the punishment wouldn't fit the crime.

I must have tried Dad's patience a thousand times in my early years, but he had never resorted to whipping me. He just wasn't the type to do it. Not even when my friend Mike and I stood on the roof of Dad's store soon afterward and dropped water balloons onto the heads of Saturday shoppers. When the complaints began surfacing, we could hear my dad shouting, "That's gotta be Tommy doing this!" The roof sloped down low enough to leap from, and I went first. The heavyset Mike followed, flattening me. He got away, and Dad got what was left of me, grabbing me by the shirttail and picking me up like a limp squirrel. When he was sure I wasn't seriously injured, he chewed me out and sent me home.

3

Trapped

Me about the time I contracted polio

❖❖❖❖❖❖❖❖❖❖❖❖❖❖❖❖❖❖❖❖❖

Sometime around the age of eight, I began waking up each morning almost too weak to get out of bed. This happened in varying degrees off and on for several years. There were times when I felt like getting into mischief, and other times I didn't feel like doing anything. Mom and Dad didn't say so, but they must have thought their crafty young son was feigning fatigue just to get out of going to school, as I had been guilty of doing on Sunday school mornings in the past. They might have been right at first. I loved hanging out with the kids, but I hated having to sit in class trying to keep up with the others. So staying at home for a while would have been enjoyable—if only I hadn't been feeling so lousy all the time. *Maybe I just need a breather,* I

19

thought. Boy, was I about to get one, and what a monster it would turn out to be.

Finally, the folks began to think perhaps there really was something wrong, and they sent me to be examined by a physician. He must have thought I had "tired blood" or something, because he prescribed a liver shot every day, along with liver pills that tasted so horrible I had to take them with a spoonful of grape jelly just to swallow them without gagging. To this day, my distaste for liver ranks right up there with former President George Bush's aversion to broccoli, and the thought of eating grape jelly turns my stomach.

After a lengthy period of shots and pills, I was still getting worse: more and more exhausted, achy all the time, nagging headache that never seemed to go away—and finally I began to have trouble breathing. These were the telltale symptoms of polio. There was an epidemic sweeping the country at the time. It had been going on for years, afflicting thousands of people all over the country—mostly kids, who were hit the worst—and a lot of those who didn't die from it went home physically impaired to varying degrees, or even paralyzed. Polio was rampant, and people were so afraid that they shunned anyone with it as if it was the plague. Not even people in the medical profession knew whether it was contagious. No one knew where it originated, how it was contracted. It was absolutely frightening.

I was sent to an isolation ward at the nearest hospital, seventy-five miles away, where they kept me under constant observation and tried every kind of treatment imaginable for the next few weeks. But nothing helped, and I kept getting worse and worse while people in adjoining beds began dying left and right. I was struggling just to take a breath when they finally put me in an iron lung, a big tank that looks like something out of an old science-fiction movie. I lay there on my back with just my head sticking out the end while a mechanical bellows forced oxygen into my lungs. For days and weeks and months I lay there in a room filled with other people in other iron lungs, each of us staring up at our own eyes in the reflection of a mirror above our heads, while we listened to the wheezing of the machines, and always somebody crying quietly in the darkness late at night. So did I, wondering if I was going to die, feeling deserted by everyone who mattered, mad at my parents, mad at God for letting this happen, mad at myself, almost crazy with loneliness and fear.

Visitors weren't permitted, of course, because we might be contagious, and the nurses weren't eager to be in our ward. When they did come in, they'd be wearing masks over their faces so that we could only see their eyes. They stayed away from us as much as possible, coming in to feed us, change the bedding, take us out now and then for a bath, and that was it. If they could, most of them avoided even touching us, and even though they tried to hide it and put up a front, I could sense their feelings. We all could.

There in my little spaceship, as I came to think of it, I couldn't look at picture books, couldn't sit up. I couldn't even scratch my nose. My only company was the others who were sick, and they were about as much fun to me as I was to them: none. Some of us did get acquainted, but there wasn't much to talk about except how it felt being trapped in our metal prisons. A few of the kids were in such bad shape they couldn't even talk, or didn't want to, and they were the ones who finally died. Most of the time I just slept and slept, constantly it seemed, and everything took on the quality of a bad dream from which I would never awaken, an endless nightmare so real, and yet so unreal, that I could hardly remember the life I'd led before I got there, let alone imagine actually getting out one day and returning to my home and my family.

I even started praying on a regular basis, mostly at night— just the prayers of a lonely child. Remembering services attended with my dad and praying in the only way I knew how, I would say things like, "God, just get me out of here and I'll be good from now on, I swear it. I promise to stop taking shortcuts. I promise to stop talking back. I promise to do what my parents tell me to do and be respectful about it—if only You'll give me another chance." I thought God was punishing me for being a bad boy.

I don't know if He was or not, but the worst was yet to come. Lying there on my back one night, I got sick and threw up all over myself. I couldn't get my hands out of the breathing machine to wipe my face, and I was afraid to call a nurse. I always felt that I was such a bother to them, and I didn't want to risk upsetting them in the middle of the night. So I just lay there all night in my own vomit.

The next morning the doctor happened to be making his rounds early. A nurse accompanying him flicked the lights on as they entered, and we all began waking up. As he started looking in on the kids by the door, one boy closer to me said, "Doctor, you better check on Tommy here. Something happened to him last night."

The physician walked right over to me wearing a surgical mask and one of those skullcaps along with his long white coat, and he bent over me, his eyes full of concern.

"Tommy," he said, "what happened to you?"

"I'm sorry," I stammered. "I didn't mean to do it."

"You didn't do anything wrong, son," he said. "My goodness, didn't someone come and help you?"

"I didn't want to bother anybody."

At that point, he must have realized the nurses weren't making their regular rounds as required and said something under his breath, then he whipped off his mask and began wiping my face, cleaning it as best he could. Picking me up, he pulled me out of the iron lung, then sat holding me on the cold hardwood floor, oblivious to the stains and the odor I had been smelling all night. I can still taste it, I can feel the way it put a sharp edge on my teeth, I can still smell the regurgitated food. But most of all, I will never forget the clean smell of that starched and pressed white coat he wore.

"You're getting your coat dirty, Doctor," I protested.

"Don't worry about that," he answered as one of the nurses came over and said, "Doctor, we'll take care of him."

"Where were you last night?" he snapped. "Why didn't you take care of this boy *then*? He'll remember this terrible experience the rest of his life! How could you do this to him? Get away from him! Get away from me!"

He was shouting by now, and when they left us, he just sat there hugging me and rocking back and forth.

Moved by this pathetic incident of neglect, he seemed to be crying as if for humanity itself, and I couldn't help but cry with him.

This great man also started talking about faith in a way I'd never heard before, explaining to me about God and how He loved all people—even me. He told me how God would watch over me and protect me if I would trust Him. He talked for a long time, and I mostly didn't understand much of what he said. But just listening to the sound of his voice as he spoke to me, *me personally*, was better than any medicine I could have been given that day. Being just a kid, I didn't fully grasp all of what he was trying to say, but I know it was the beginning of my realization of how important faith in God is to our lives. If I have any good at all in me today, it began right there at that moment with a gentle, loving touch and a caring heart.

You know something? The doctor was right about that incident. I have remembered it—and him—and will for the rest of my life. I know that the nurses were not really uncaring. They tried, and I can now understand their hesitancy about touching us. Fear can paralyze us, but we cannot let it stand in the way of our compassion for those who need us the most. But more than the pain and humiliation of that awful experience, I remember being hugged by a compassionate human being, and that's why I believe in hugs today. Hugs not drugs, hugs not hurt, hugs not hate.

What happened not long afterward might have been just a coincidence, but perhaps it was something else, something more spiritual. One morning it dawned on me that my breathing was coming just a little easier than it had in a long time. Hope crept in and gradually replaced fear, anger, and frustration. And with that hope, unknown to me at the time, maybe some of my hardheaded German determination kicked in. Over the next few weeks, my attitude brightened as I realized I was actually getting better. It didn't occur to me at the time, but over the years I would come to understand it wasn't the iron lung that brought me back to life again. It was the touch of the doctor, one of the kindest people I can remember, who had cradled a young boy's head with loving hands and seemed not to mind the distasteful task of wiping and cleaning his face for him. Isn't that all any of us really need? The breath of life, the breath of love to give us hope and faith. If that wasn't an act of God, I'll never know one.

That hug was just a sample of the welcome I knew would be waiting for me when I was finally well and released to go home. A month or so later, my parents were told they could take me back to Lakeview. I had spent many months inside that apparatus, and now I was bidding it good-bye and returning at last to Mom and Dad. Wow! I thought I would burst with excitement. Mom and Dad finally arrived to pick me up, and there we were—just hugging and laughing and crying and talking all at once. Then we left for home. *Home*. From that moment, the word took on new meaning for me.

I had been rolled out in a wheelchair, but I felt like a bird set free from a cage, soaring through the sky. I was *free*! At last I could begin life anew. It was an indescribable thrill. Gazing out the car window as we sped northward along old Highway 46 headed for Lakeview, I drank it all in—the trees, the grass, and the sky, the fragrance of flowers and fresh-turned earth, eager to experience everything; it was a feeling I'd never lose. It was springtime in Michigan, and in Tommy Harken's heart.

At home, Mom had prepared a feast fit for a king—at least I thought so, because I felt like one. It was a favorite dish, then and now: garden-fresh peas with potatoes and white gravy. Wow! I really *was* home. Later, I entered my own room, slowly at first after so long away. Gradually it engulfed me, welcomed me back, fell into place. I lay across my wonderful old bed, and surrounded by the familiar things a kid loves, I slept the peaceful sleep of the innocent, probably for the last time.

Two days later, after conducting a few more tests, the local doctor came to our house accompanied by county health department staff and suggested that my mother call my father at his store and ask him to come home immediately.

Me, Melba, and my granddaughter McKenzie visit the house where I was quarantined with tuberculosis.

They had something to discuss with both Mom and Dad. I didn't know *what* was about to happen. Dad's store was just a couple of blocks away, and when he arrived a few minutes later, the doctor told them I had been diagnosed with tuberculosis. *Tuberculosis* was a big word. Still is. I couldn't even pronounce it, and I definitely had no idea what it was. But whatever it was, it didn't sound good to me.

Thankfully, it was a light case, not bad enough to hospitalize me again, but I would have to be quarantined at home, probably for some time, they said. They placed a big sign by the front door before they left. They'd had it with them when they arrived. I remember that it was bright yellow with big black letters: QUARANTINED—as highly visible and recognizable in those days as Shell Oil signs are today. That meant the premises had to be vacated immediately, with no one allowed to come and go. TB was as infectious then as it is today, and my father and brother had to move out. Dad checked into the local hotel, and my brother stayed at a neighbor's house. My mother would have to take her chances at home, because somebody had to take care of me—again.

I couldn't believe it. I'd been through so much that at first I was almost beyond shock and disappointment. The door wasn't locked, but it might as well have been, because I wasn't allowed to leave my room. "Doctor's orders," my mom would say, trying to sound cheerful. Three times a day, she would leave a plate of food outside the door. She brought fresh towels, bedding, and sleepwear every day, and she was always asking if I needed anything.

Yeah, I would think to myself, *I need to get out of here*—but I tried not to complain. My folks were doing everything they could do for me. For a while it wasn't so bad. But as the weeks dragged by, it became an ordeal almost as unbearable as the time I had spent in the hospital. I had simply moved from the iron lung into a larger cell. It was comfortably furnished with all my belongings, but a cell nevertheless. A big old Philco radio helped me pass the time listening to episodes of *The Green Hornet* and *The Shadow.* These seemed more real than life in the outside world, so close but so far away. It was eerie, like watching a movie with no sound. I felt like a ghost haunting my own home. Kids from school would ride their bikes or walk by, but always on the other side of the street. Only one friend had the nerve to approach my window and visit for a moment or two. Thanks, Ben.

Watching my brother from my window while I was quarantined, I wished I could get out of my room, which had become a prison cell.

❖❖❖❖❖❖❖❖❖❖❖❖❖❖❖❖❖❖❖❖❖❖❖❖❖❖❖❖❖❖❖❖❖

"Hi, Tommy. Are you gonna get better?" he'd ask.

"I dunno, I hope so," I'd answer, and he'd be gone.

Once, on a Sunday afternoon during the coldest part of winter, my mother went to a neighbor's house for a few minutes, and I sneaked out of my room. Walking around the house for that few brief moments, I felt like a prisoner who had broken out. Standing at a kitchen window, I watched as my dad skated on the frozen lake with kids from the town, some of them friends of mine. I could actually *feel* the pain of not being with them. Dad, of course, had a right to some kind of recreation and enjoyment. I knew that, but at the same time I resented it, and once again I questioned God about it, asking Him why, why, why? God's answer for the time being was silence.

While Dad was out on the ice, he happened to be pulling a boy on a sled and made a sudden turn and caught his foot in a crack in the ice. It broke his leg. For a long time after it happened, I thought I was somehow responsible because of the anger I had felt.

In this strange limbo, I soon lost track of time, but when the doctor arrived at the house one day for his weekly visit, I woke up from it with a shock. He went through his routine with the stethoscope, but this time, instead of the usual "hmm" and slow shaking of his head, he brightened and placed the listening devices into my own ears. "Listen, Tommy," he said excitedly, pressing the cold tip back on my chest.

Scared, thinking I must be a goner then and there, I did as I was told, and it sounded like a wind tunnel in there. I was sure it was the final death rattle.

But with a big smile, he clapped me on the shoulder and said, "Clear! It's clear, Tommy! The congestion is gone!"

I couldn't believe my ears. I found myself being cautious. I had been through the excitement of getting out of the hospital, only to have my hopes fade. I'd experienced false alarms and disappointments before, and this seemed too good to be true. I had felt it all, from the happy optimism of going home to finding that all was not well. So I figured it wasn't. The doubt I was feeling must have shown on my face, because the doctor read my thoughts, and looking at me sincerely, he said, "I promise you, Tommy, you're completely free of infection. You're going to be all right." How I wanted to believe him, and my heart raced with excitement when he added, "You can go back to school!"

I could go back to school? After years of being sick at home, then all that time in the hospital and being out of school sick at home for what seemed like forever, now the doctor was saying I could go back. It was almost as if I'd never gone in the first place. Yet, I wanted nothing more than to be a normal kid again, to return to my old life and pick up where I had left off. But I had now missed many school terms, and on the day I went back to class, I felt like a complete stranger among kids I was growing up with. I was thrust into the seventh grade as if I hadn't missed a day, and to tell the truth, I couldn't remember a complete year of schooling.

As I entered the classroom, all eyes turned toward me. "Well, Tommy," said the teacher, standing at the blackboard and poised to write, "I hear you've been a little bit sick."

"Yes, sir," I said quietly, lowering my eyes and sliding into the nearest empty seat. Staring at the desktop, I wished everybody would just ignore me until I got used to the idea of being back.

But they were still looking at me when the teacher cleared his throat and said, "Tommy, come on up here and show us what you learned while you were goofing off."

My face flushed bright red as I shuffled to the front of the room. The other kids were whispering and snickering among themselves, because they knew I had always been a little slow. I think my parents knew it, too, and so did the faculty at school, but as I mentioned before, in those days there wasn't much awareness about learning disabilities, and nobody really knew what to do with people like me. By the time I started getting sick, unable to read for whatever reason, I felt angry and left out because seldom was I well enough to ride my bike or play ball with the others. So I began to feel completely cut off from everything I cared about.

Back in front of my old class after so long, I felt even more cut off than before, completely alone and out of place. And at this particular moment, almost scared to death.

"Grab that chalk there," said the teacher. "Let's see how your spelling is. I'll make it easy for you . . . spell *cat*."

All I could do was look at him and say, "Uhhh . . ."

"I said spell *cat*, Tommy."

I was so flustered I broke the chalk, but I couldn't write a single letter.

Finally, in exasperation, he said, "Just go sit down," and I skulked back to my seat in shame.

While the teacher turned back toward the blackboard, the guy behind me whispered, "Tom, it's C-A-T."

"I know that!" I snapped over my shoulder. "I just couldn't think up there."

With the other kids laughing aloud, the laughter piercing my soul, the teacher whirled around angrily at the disruption and impulsively hurled an eraser at me. It missed, but I was beyond humiliation.

"We've heard quite enough from you today, young man!" he said.

I didn't say another word for the rest of the class, and that night I walked home numb with shock. A couple of weeks went by, and it was all downhill for me. I just couldn't seem to get the hang of anything. My only comfort was that I could still play basketball with the other boys at school. I wasn't on the team, but they'd always let me hang around and work out with them anyway. And now that I was well enough to join them again, I could hardly wait to get out on the floor. They were taking a road trip to play a game at another school the next day, so I was there that evening and hopped on the bus with the others. We were about to leave when the coach looked over, saw me, and asked me to step off with him for a minute.

"Tommy," he said quietly, "the principal says your grades are going to have to improve before we can let you go with us anymore. I'm sorry."

He patted me on the shoulder, gave me a quick hug, and as I looked painfully up at him, I could see in his eyes that he felt the same way. He got back inside as the driver started the engine. The coach liked me and truly was hurt. Many years later, our paths would cross, and he would tell me how he really hadn't wanted to do it, but orders were orders. I couldn't know this that evening as a couple of the guys waved good-bye and the bus rolled out of sight without me. I can still see the snow falling and the streetlights coming on as I walked slowly homeward with tears streaming down my face, alone again.

Something inside me seemed to die that night. *They've taken away the one thing I really know how to do,* I thought to myself—*the only thing I love—basketball.*

"That's it!" I shouted into the darkness. "I'm never going back."

The love of basketball would fade as I grew up, and many things in life would take its place. But I never went back to class again.

4

"God Has a Plan for You"

Me about the time I dropped out of seventh grade
❖❖❖❖❖❖❖❖❖❖❖❖❖❖❖❖❖❖❖❖❖❖❖

I tried to hold back the tears when I broke the news to my parents that night. But it was no use. I had promised God to be a good boy if only He would spare me from polio and let me return to my life at home. Then He had tested my faith again, and that time I was imprisoned in my own bedroom, stricken with tuberculosis. Set free again, I had returned at last to school, only to discover that I was too far behind to catch up. I was cut off, shut out of everything I knew and loved. I felt lost, betrayed.

"I don't know what I was cut out for," I told Mom and Dad, sobbing, "but it sure isn't book-learning." I expected them to lay down the law and order me back to school, but they knew

I'd always had a hard time keeping up, and I guess the news came as no surprise to them.

Mom put her arms around me and said, "Don't worry. Everything's going to be all right." I'm sure she didn't believe it, and neither did I, but Dad took me aside, and I've never forgotten what he told me.

"Tommy," he said with deep feeling, "you've had a rotten deal in life so far. But sooner or later you're going to make it in this world. You've got to believe that God has a plan for you, and He knows what He's doing. You're a good worker, and you're not afraid of hard work, but you're going to have to work harder than most people do. And one day you've got to marry a smart woman."

It took me a while to understand fully the wisdom of his advice about marrying the right kind of woman. But I didn't waste any time rolling up my sleeves and going to work when he offered me a full-time job at the store. By the time the door opened every morning, I had already swept up inside and out front, and I had restocked the shelves with merchandise, ready to greet the first customer of the day. I went back to my old job, ringing up sales at the cash register, bagging them, and carrying them outside.

But I also taught myself a new job. I had to, because it involved taking orders on the phone, and I couldn't read or write. I dreaded hearing that telephone ring. I could work day and night and fight a grizzly bear in between, but the one thing I wanted to run away from was that darn telephone. In my mind it took on a life of its own just for the purpose of tormenting me. It seemed to know I couldn't read or write and took pleasure in making me sweat.

"Tommy, catch that," my dad would say, knowing I was good with the customers and turning a deaf ear when the phone rang. Usually it was someone wanting to pick up an order on the way home from work. These customers would be in a hurry, so I had to get my brain in gear and listen fast as they recited their shopping lists: Del Monte green beans, Libby whole-kernel corn, Post Toasties, Skinner's Raisin Bran, or a thousand other items. I didn't realize it at the time, but those phone orders, one by one, were providing me with a valuable alternative for the education I was missing. I was being forced to compartmentalize my brain and develop an exhaustive memory. There was plenty of vacant space in there, so develop it I did.

I started out feeling that the more I chatted with callers, the more stuff they'd think of to order, so I'd cut the conversation to a bare minimum. I must have sounded brusque to some of them. "Is this Tommy?" they would say, missing my usual joshing. "Tommy Harken?" I didn't know or care if I was hurting the store's sales figures, but after a while, I got better at remembering orders, and I began to enjoy myself, getting back into my playful mode and keeping customers on the phone, prodding them to order more.

I'd speed through the aisles repeating the names of all the items they'd ordered while plucking them from the shelves. By this time I had memorized the colors or the pictures on the labels, so it didn't take me long to fill the order and get it ready for checkout. If Dad was behind the meat case, I'd relay those orders to him and make a pass by the freezer to snatch the ice cream last. Very seldom did I miss an item, and then it was likely to be some feminine product. In the first place, I was unfamiliar with them, and requests for particular products were related to me in veiled phrases, as dictated by the times.

Dad and I worked well together, and for the most part he was pleased that I had come to work for him. For one thing, he had a helper, and that meant menial duties fell to me. In my mind, working in the butcher-shop area ranked somewhere below sweeping and pulling old products to the front of the shelves. Since Dad didn't like it any more than I did, guess who got the job? But he would help me do some of the heavy work, and he was a patient teacher.

He would lift those big hindquarters with one hand, taking them off the hooks and plopping them across the sturdy meat block—which had to be scraped clean daily—so that I could begin the laborious job of turning the massive slabs of meat into neat steaks and chops that would soon be served at supper tables all over Lakeview. It was a never-ending task I could barely keep up with, and there was more to do besides. Once the slicing was finished, there was boning of the necks to carve out every last ounce of edible meat for sale. That was one tough job, and I hated it. First, it was boring, and second, it represented pennies when I compared it to what I could be doing. But this had to be done, too, along with grinding meat for hamburger and sausage. I learned from the competition that you could add to the weight—and make more money for it—by adding water to the meat. So I tried the water trick, thinking Dad would be pleased that I was increasing profits for the store. But he gave me a lecture instead.

"We don't cut corners to make money," he said, and that made me feel small.

I knew he was right, but I hadn't matured enough to appreciate what he was telling me. Still, I kept trying to earn his approval, and on one occasion, when he and my mother were off enjoying the only vacation they ever took, I strayed unintentionally from the straight and narrow again. My brother and I had been left in charge of the store, entrusted with the very livelihood of the Harken family. Having a couple of years' seniority, my brother could choose to man the register, so I was relegated to my customary duties. But with Dad out of the picture for a while, my entrepreneurial spirit reared its irrepressible head and looked around for something to do that would make a good impression and maybe even garner a nod of approval from Dad when he got home.

In the tiny back storeroom was a truckload of Hills Bros. coffee. It had been delivered one day when I was away on an errand, and I hadn't paid much attention to it until now. Figuring there must have been some mistake in shipping, and Dad was stuck with the whole consignment, I decided to solve the problem for him by selling every last pound before he returned from his trip. Over my brother's objections, I put the entire shipment on sale, setting up beautiful displays all over the store. Customers bought ten, twelve, fifteen cans at a time, and I thought I was hitting a home run for the Harken team. After four or five days, every last one was sold. I was really proud of myself.

When the folks finally got home, happy to see the house and the store still standing, they enjoyed a moment of tranquillity before I broke the good news that I'd sold all the coffee and made more space in the storeroom.

"Why in the world did you do that?" my father asked incredulously.

"I thought you'd be glad I sold it."

"Tommy," he said patiently, "I bought all that coffee in anticipation of a price increase, so that we could make more money on it later when the retail market goes up."

"But isn't that a shortcut?" I asked. "You said we shouldn't cut corners."

"No, son, it's called an educated guess. You have a lot to learn about doing business."

I never tried to sell coffee again. In fact, I never learned how to make coffee. I left that to someone else and concentrated on becoming successful at making money. That was the last time I went out of my way to impress Dad with my business savvy. It seemed to me that no matter what I did, first at home, then at the store, he was going to disapprove anyway, so I guess I decided to stop trying and start taking every shortcut in sight. But even at my worst, he was never that tough on me. In most ways, he was a very understanding and loving father. I just happened to be the son who didn't follow the rules and do what he was told. For some reason, I always took the other route. I could go with the flow, but it was more fun to make a few waves.

My favorite soft drink in those days was Coca-Cola, so I always gave it better display space than any other brand—until my father explained with some annoyance that Nehi was a more profitable item because the bottler offered him a better price. I hated being scolded again, so I decided to take my revenge—on Nehi. When the distributors assigned me the job of separating empty deposit bottles for pickup, I decided to sell a few cases of empties to a friend of mine who worked at another store. When my father found out about it, of course, he pitched a fit—not only because I kept the deposit income, but because the Nehi man, who had seven or eight kids, had bought all his groceries from Dad until that incident, and now he had taken his business elsewhere. "You have to treat your vendors the same as customers," said Dad. "I hope you learn that some day." That was good advice, of course, but I wasn't ready to take it.

What I was ready for was a change of scenery. After a long year for both of us at the store, I walked into the house one evening after work and announced that a friend of mine and I were going to take a trip to Florida in May.

"No way," my mother replied instantly.

"Sure we can, it'll be fun. Dad understands. He'll agree to it, right, Dad?" He didn't answer.

"You're only fourteen," Mom persisted.

"Fourteen and a half. And Ben is almost sixteen."

"How would you get there?" asked Dad.

"Hitchhike."

Back in those days, there was no stigma attached to hitchhiking, especially for young guys like us. It was still a safe way to travel for people who didn't have any other way to get around.

They looked at each other, then at me, and shrugged. Both of them knew we'd be going whether they gave us their permission or not, so they gave me their blessings and were probably even relieved to be free of me for a while. They and Ben's parents even wrote notes stating "to whom it may concern" that we weren't runaways, just in case any law enforcement officials questioned us on the road.

Packing a couple of cheap old suitcases with a change of shirts and jeans, along with fresh socks, underwear, a toothbrush, and twenty dollars each for spending money, we went out to Highway 46, stuck out our thumbs and, like clockwork, a huge eighteen-wheeler pulled up in a hiss of air brakes. Climbing up to the cab, we slid in beside the driver and hit the road, beside ourselves with excitement. It was the first time I'd ever ridden in one of those monsters. I loved it, but not until the driver taught me how to avoid having my bones jarred every time we hit a bump. Once I knew to relax and not brace myself, the truck seat and I got along just fine. Five hours and three hundred miles later, he let us off in Wooster, Ohio. There was no turning back now, with the open road stretching out before us beyond the horizon, endless miles of countryside passing by in a blur of farms and towns as we made our way southeast.

Soaking up the local color as we stood beside the road waiting for the next ride, we lived a lifetime of adventure in the next few weeks, befriending farmers and fellow travelers, sleeping on motel lawn furniture until we were chased off at dawn. We were halfway through South Carolina—riding in the back of a chicken truck—when a fast-talking character in a brand-new Cadillac picked us up and chauffeured us all the way to Florida, driving like mad. We were so happy to be out of sight, and odor, of those chickens, we didn't even squawk when he made the tires squeal going around those mountainous curves and hills. The flamboyant gent said he owned a fleet of banana boats and asked us to come work for him, but when we said thanks anyway, he dropped us off, and we went back on the thumb for the rest of our trip south. Then, and many times since, I have wondered how life would've turned out had I decided to seek my fate and fortune on the banana boats.

Ben and I also wondered if we'd gotten out of the Cadillac too soon when we found ourselves on foot, passing a chain gang alongside the road. Much to the amusement of the yelling guards, several of the convicts growled and grabbed at us as we ran by them as fast as we could go. We knew we had arrived at our destination when we hit the outskirts of Fort Lauderdale, and we had one ace in the hole. Mr. Beech, his real name by the way, from back home had a winter place here, and he hadn't yet left to return to Lakeview and his appliance center. He had jokingly told us boys to drop in for a visit if we ever made it to Florida, never believing we would. Well, here we were, and was he surprised to see us. But he welcomed us, and when the brief visit ended, he even handed both of us some cash and told us to enjoy ourselves but to be careful. Then, as I would learn later, he went back into the house and notified our parents that we were all right. Ben and I took in a few sights, then beachcombed in paradise for a week or so. We caddied at a local course for food money, played golf and tennis, and I met a cute blonde tennis player who found me a willing student. For a very nominal amount, an old lady in a boardinghouse took us in and fed us for a few days; she thought we were great kids. And then, finally and reluctantly, we thumbed our way back home again, taking our sweet time about it.

We made the whole three thousand miles in exactly 101 rides, and every one of them was a story we'd remember for the rest of our lives. My parents were relieved to see me safe and sound, embracing me and even shedding a few tears of joy—but they were ready to burn me at the stake for waiting to get in touch with them until I walked back in the front door after three weeks away. If not for Mr. Beech's call, they'd probably have put out an all-points bulletin for us. They hadn't believed we'd get much beyond the outskirts of Lakeview. But we were the toasts of the town, small though it was. Ben and I even got invited to tea parties, where the ladies wanted to hear all about our travels and adventures—not believing our parents had allowed it. Our answer was simple and direct: They wouldn't have if they'd known we might make it.

It was wonderful to be home—until I got a load of my white cocker spaniel, Skeet, who greeted me after rolling in the wet tar that was being used to blacktop the street outside our house. He looked like a sticky black cocker spaniel. I raised such a ruckus with my parents for allowing this to happen while I was away that they probably wished I'd turn around and go back to Florida.

I almost did. After trying to go back to work at my father's store for several months, we both realized it wasn't going to work. Even if he and I hadn't been rubbing each other the wrong way, both of us knew we eventually would, and the final straw finally popped out in the form of another of my impulsive actions. I had struck up a relationship with a girl who was causing both Mom and Dad deep concern because of my youth. She was an attractive young Lakeview lady, and she was working as a carhop when we began dating. She was seventeen, two years older than I was, but I was mature for my age, and we hit it off. She loved listening to my line of bull, and I could sure dish it out.

"Let's get married," I blurted out one night, and before either of us knew what was happening we had "run away" to Elkhart, Indiana, and were man and wife. Wow! I was fifteen.

"I can't tell you how to live your life, Tommy," Dad said. "Your mother and I think you've made a big mistake. You're far too young for such a serious relationship. But since you insist on making your own decisions, you'll just have to live with them. We love you, and we want nothing but the best for you, but we think it's time for you to set out on your own."

He was as kind about it as he could be, but the bottom line was that they wanted me to quit my job, leave home, and get out of town. I was stunned, but when he went on to talk about the doors he planned to open for me, I could hardly wait to leave. Dad had heard from the Nehi route man—the one whose empties I had sold to another market—that there was a job available in the produce department at a Kroger grocery store in Greenville, twenty-five miles northwest of Lakeview. By then, I had an old junker of a car, a 1936 something-or-other that would get me to and from work. It was a win-win situation, as I saw it. I was glad to be leaving, and my parents were probably glad to be rid of me.

My new wife and I got an apartment, set up housekeeping together, and I almost found myself getting serious and planning for the future. I was making a dollar an hour. At the store, I worked in produce, stocked shelves, anything that needed doing. I was a worker, with energy to spare. When the produce manager at Kroger's quit to go to work for Meijers grocery store nearby, he wanted to take me with him because he knew I wouldn't back off from anything, no matter how difficult it might appear. But I still wasn't earning enough to support two, let alone a family. My wife supplemented our income with another drive-in job until our first son was born.

Some time later, Bob Cahill told me he was joining the service, so thinking I could better myself and somehow maybe even finish my education, I decided to enlist in the U.S. Air Force. Lying about my age and my education, I had no problem getting in. The enlistment officer needed to meet his quota, and I was another warm body. He and Bob even filled out the papers. It wasn't long before I was shipped off for basic training at New York State's Sampson Air Force Base.

My wife visited me at Sampson once, over a weekend, riding up with Bob's mother when she came to see him. It wasn't long until we were expectant parents.

I fit right into the regimented military discipline, but the air force soon discovered that my education left a great deal to be desired. I failed all the required IQ tests, but rather than bust me out, I was assigned to the permanent one-O classification, which I learned years later is reserved for those who are considered uneducable and untrainable in virtually every capacity.

Tom Harken of the United States Air Police
I was only seventeen when I joined up, but I was big enough
for recruiters.

❖❖❖❖❖❖❖❖❖❖❖❖❖❖❖❖❖❖❖❖❖❖❖❖❖

When my "training" was complete, I was given two weeks' leave and told to report to Oklahoma's Altus Air Force Base. Somehow I had acquired a rather new 1953 Dodge, and we had to have somewhere to live, so in Michigan I bought a seventeen-and-a-half-foot LaSalle travel trailer, and we began our trek. It's a miracle we didn't have some sort of wreck, and that we made it at all, since I drove at a crawl most of the way. There I was, not even out of my teens—first-time husband, expectant father, and first-time trailer puller.

But eventually we arrived in Oklahoma, and I parked our

new home at a trailer park near the Strategic Air Command base under General Curtis Lemay.

Uneducated as I was, the air force didn't know what to do with me. But they did find a couple of more responsible jobs for me during my stay—in munitions and in the air police. But the pay was marginal, especially after the birth of our second son, and the four of us had to live together in that tiny trailer. Then, having been unable to meet any of the notes, my car was repossessed and taken all the way back to Michigan.

So, there in the mid-'50s, and even with the poorhouse beckoning, I was able to obtain something I'd wanted since 1946—a 1946 Cushman motor scooter. That's what I rode to and from the base, and to supplement my income, I was selling Mason shoes to anyone who was willing to put down a deposit and wait until they were shipped. Relying on my old line of bull, I'd gab while my customer filled out his name and address. The $2.50 or $3.00 deposit was my commission, and every little bit helped.

We were still struggling when I met a guy who sold vacuum cleaners. It was a bigger-ticket item, and he offered to show me how to sell them. When he decided to change brands and sell Kirby vacuum cleaners, commission potential was thirty dollars each. That sounded like a better deal than selling shoes, so I went to one of the meetings with him. That's when I met Casey Southern, the salesman's salesman. I would learn a lot from him, but early on I realized it was even harder to sell a vacuum cleaner than it was to sell shoes door-to-door—and more paper for someone to fill out. Besides, it took me away from home at night, even on weekends, and the expected extra income wasn't coming in.

Once more, I somehow acquired another car to drive, and I really tried to make sales, but it was at this time that my wife and I realized our marriage wouldn't work. We were children trying to raise children, and the emotional strain began to take its toll on the relationship. It was no one's fault in particular.

Money was always short, and we argued a lot. She would cry, the babies would cry, and I'd storm out the door.

One Christmas Eve, when I should have been home with them by our little tree, I was out knocking on doors and trying to sell enough shoes or vacuum cleaners to put a few presents underneath it. Catching the holiday spirit, most people opened the door, and I could smell turkey cooking and hear carols playing while a few of them gave me candy canes or an extra apple for the stocking. At one house, I thought I had a vac sold, but at the last minute they changed their minds and said, "No thanks, but have a very merry Christmas and a happy New Year." Yeah, right.

Nobody even needed fan belts or small parts from me that night, and the lights in our living room were dark when I got back home at midnight. My wife's response to my statement that I hadn't lucked into a sale was, "I knew you couldn't sell those things anyway."

Neither one of us wanted to face it, but the next morning I woke up knowing that no matter how hard we tried, it wasn't going to work out. At that moment I don't know which emotion I felt more intensely, rage or despair, but bitter words were spoken by both of us, and that night after my late shift at the camp, I returned home to find a bare spot where the trailer had been and all my clothes thrown around the yard. It was all over, and it was raining. (One of my sons from that marriage now works for me. The other lives far away, but we sometimes exchange cards at Christmas.)

Blindly, I drove over to the nearest liquor store and bought a couple of bottles of cheap booze—Ten High. It was all I could afford. Other than a few beers now and then, I had never been much of a drinker, but I intended to make up for lost time. Driving out to a deserted cotton field, I leaned up against the car, opened the first bottle, and started trying to figure out what had happened to my life. By the next morning I was sleeping it off and AWOL. A farmer found me in his field and called the air base. The air police sergeant came to my aid, and once I told him what had happened—the whole story—he voiced his understanding, then filled out the necessary paperwork that would assign me back into the barracks. I remember feeling grateful that the pain in my head was pounding too hard for me to be able to feel the pain in my heart.

"Where do I go from here?" I said aloud to no one in particular. I was only twenty, but I felt that my life was already over.

5

Miss Melba

*I got set up on a date with this beautiful woman.
Boy, did I get lucky!*

❖❖❖❖❖❖❖❖❖❖❖❖❖❖❖❖❖❖❖❖❖❖❖❖

➤ Boy, was I wrong. Life was really about to *begin* for me, and it's a good thing I didn't know it. I probably would have totally messed things up. I almost did anyway.

My best friend at the time, a fellow air policeman by the name of Lucky Simpson, was going steady with Janny Shockley. Lucky was an Airman 1st Class, which at the time was signified by three stripes. I, of course, still wore my single stripe. It was all I'd ever have, but I was stuck with it. Janny was a local girl and something of a matchmaker. Matchmakers, bless them, are a breed of their own, and if not for these perceptive people, the world might not be as well populated as it is today. They just seem to have a way of knowing when two people are a *match* for each other.

By the late '50s, the act of "going steady" had become a catchphrase for young couples who weren't ready to be married but had a yen to settle in temporarily with someone who just might be "the one." It was the result of an official proposal, usually by the boy, to date someone on a regular basis, excluding most all others, for better or worse as far as the usual teenage trials and tribulations were concerned.

"Well, me and my baby are goin' steady," went a tremendously popular song by Faron Young. The term eventually crept into the vocabularies of the older generation.

"We ain't married, but we're gettin' ready to tie the knot, and I'm gonna make her my own."

Tying the knot supposedly signified cinching the deal forever. Going steady left you with an easy out that the more binding term, *engaged*, didn't allow.

For some reason, Lucky's steady, Janny, decided she should introduce me to *her* best friend, a beautiful, statuesque blonde she thought I'd go for in a big way.

Call it luck or call it fate, but at the time I was in no mood for any kind of date even with the looker she described. She was a civilian working in an office right there on the base, and any other time this would've been right up my alley. But because of recent circumstances, I wasn't ready to come around to that quite yet.

"She's nice, Tommy. You really should meet her," Janny urged one day when I ran into her and Lucky somewhere. "She's just right for you. I think the two of you should get together."

That's all I needed. Me, Hotlips Harken, getting together with Miss *Nice*.

"She even plays basketball, Tommy," Lucky said convincingly. "You love basketball, and she was a star on her high school team. In fact, she was the captain of the all-star team."

"Yeah, I coulda been a basketball star too," I said, sinking into the only comfortable defense of my uneducated existence—resentment and sarcasm.

Janny didn't know how to take that, but Lucky passed over it, as friends will do, and urged me to "loosen up," as he put it.

"Loosen up" isn't in the vocabulary of anyone over the age of six who can't read and write, but to appease my friends, I put on a happy face while inwardly vowing to remain solitary and single.

All that changed when I ran into Lucky and his girlfriend a few nights later at the only nightspot in Altus, Oklahoma—the Pink Elephant, located just outside the air force base. There, sitting with Lucky and Janny, was the prettiest girl I'd ever seen.

"Tommy," said the fun-loving Janny with a wink and a knowing smile, "I'd like you to meet my very best friend in the world, Melba Curtis. This is the gal I was telling you about."

To say there was something special about this girl would be putting it mildly. I don't remember what I said, but all I could think was *Wow!*

"Janny tells me you're a real character," said Melba, smiling with a slightly amused air.

"Is that good or bad?" I asked, thinking fast.

"I don't know yet."

Whoa! This one had spunk! And she could slam-dunk too? Then and there, I was ready to start our own basketball team. Something about her made me feel really at ease for the first time in my life, and at the same time caused my skin to tingle all over. Janny and Lucky sat there smugly, happy as clams, with I-told-you-so grins on their faces. I'd never been shy, but at this moment, if my life had depended upon it, I couldn't have kept from blushing. This girl was reading my mind, or what there was left of it, and I was still trying to remember my name. *This can't be happening,* I kept thinking.

After a few minutes of chitchat, I managed a stale opener by asking, "Why don't we step outside for a breath of fresh air?" I'd heard it in a movie somewhere and thought it sounded debonair.

The humorous look on her face told me I could have done better than a lame remark like that, but she acquiesced and stood to accompany me anyway. Wow again.

Recovering my composure and gesturing with a hand, I muttered something about showing her "my new Cadillac." It was a 1958 Plymouth designed by Chrysler to resemble as closely as possible the upsweeping fins on the Cadillacs of the day. But Lucky had said Melba was a simple country girl right off the farm, so I figured she'd never know the difference. She did, and she told me so, but I wasn't fazed. More important, neither was she. In that dark parking lot where the mudholes were filled in with bottle caps, we stood there and laughed together for the first time. It felt good, felt right. Opening the door, I invited her to "try it on for size." Was I smooth, or what? Amy Vanderbilt would have been proud.

For the next hour or so, we sat in the car and talked, just getting acquainted. I shared her interest in basketball—at least I could talk about *that*—and neither of us was a stranger to hard work. She spoke of growing up on a dust-bowl cotton farm in southwestern Oklahoma, the eighth of ten children, all of them pitching in to help make a go of the place. I told her about Michigan and working in my father's store from the time I was seven. She thought Lakeview sounded a lot more picturesque than the drab surroundings she remembered.

I even ventured so far as to tell her about being a sickly kid and my long absence from school, omitting the part about dropping out.

But somehow, Melba and I found a common bond that

night. Violins didn't play, and trumpets didn't blare, but there was music in the air as if from the stars themselves. I'd never met anyone so warm, so understanding. I will admit now that I was a bit intimidated by what Janny and Lucky had told me about how bright she was, but she seemed perfectly normal to me. Dad had said I'd better marry a smart woman, and though I wasn't thinking of anything along those lines, it couldn't hurt to start looking for one.

We sat there in the front seat of that Plymouth and talked and talked. It grew late, and by whatever time it was, I was holding her hand.

Poets and songwriters have always written about the magic of a first meeting between two people destined to be together, but I didn't know a thing about that. I just knew that I had never felt this way before—a deep stirring of excitement along with a special warmth and rightness that made me realize this was something that was meant to be. I could tell she felt it too. But suddenly, as if she sensed fear, she said, "It's getting late. We have to go." The firmness with which she said it startled me, and I wondered what I had done. I figured I had carried on too much about all my crazy dreams for the future and it had turned her off. Whatever, I drove her home without a word.

At the door, I awkwardly mentioned that I'd like to see her again.

"Well," Miss Melba said, "we'll see."

Much later she would tell me what had happened—that she, too, had felt the excitement and her common sense kicked in and said, "It's time to go."

Anyway, she wasn't too sure about me, but when she didn't hear from me for about three weeks, it kind of intrigued her that I hadn't called back the next day. So she was excited when she came home from work one day and the landlady told her she had gotten a message from a guy named Tom. She tried to call Janny, but she was out, so Miss Melba dialed Lucky and told him she'd gotten a call from me but that I hadn't left my number.

Lucky said, "Hang on a second," and suddenly, I was on the line. I'd been standing right there. I was sure she'd never want to lay eyes on me again, but Lucky and I picked up Janny and went over to Melba's, and the four of us went for a drive. Later, Melba agreed to accompany me to a double feature at the drive-in. The movies that night weren't very good; it didn't matter. And the cheeseburgers we shared at the diner afterward weren't anything to write home about. I teased her for being totally unaware of cheeseburgers, much less how good they were. But this was an epic evening, because I began to open up to her about my life.

My life was looking up—at least on the social side. On the economic side, it was getting worse. I was three payments behind on my car, and the finance company that carried my note informed me that was the limit. They would have to repossess my car. The Altus Plymouth dealer's tow truck went into service. Within a matter of minutes, I was officially walking. I had about forty cents in my pocket, and that was it. That afternoon, I was out with Melba, driving Lucky's car, and the embarrassment of it all had grown so intense that I decided to stop at a pay phone, call my father, and ask him for a three-hundred-dollar loan to bail my car out. I had never asked him for a penny, but because I hadn't faced up to my responsibilities, he flatly refused me. It was humiliating, to say the least. I got back into the car, and Melba asked me what was wrong. I told her.

"Well, let's just see what we can figure out," she said. "Maybe we could go to my bank . . . Yes, I bet we could! I know the banker, and he likes me!"

"No, no, no, I can't let you do that," I protested.

"Yes!" she said. "My dad's been doing business with him for years."

"Do you really think that's a good idea?" I asked.

"Yes," she insisted. "Let's just do it."

This woman had confidence, capability, and more important, she had heart. I was totally and utterly flabbergasted.

In the first place, I was extremely pleased and impressed, not only that she was *able* to help me but also that she was *willing* to help me. I didn't know many people who could afford to be generous, and I most certainly wasn't accustomed to fits of unselfishness in anyone. But even with the wind knocked out of my sails from everything that had been happening, I still had enough red-blooded American male in me to be chagrined about accepting any form of aid, especially from a woman, but actually from anyone at all. *This lady must have a lot of faith in me!*

I used that last forty cents jingling in my pocket to buy a couple of gallons of gas for Lucky's car, and we trundled off toward tiny Roosevelt, eastward on Highway 62, then north on 183. Thirty-one miles later, we cruised into town and headed for the bank. It wasn't hard to find. The population of Roosevelt was about 250, not counting dogs and cats.

The First State Bank was located in an old-fashioned building that stood as solid as the dusty concrete corner it was built on. We parked and went inside. The old-fashioned teller's cages looked like jail cells, and bank president and owner Carl Smelser looked right through me. I expected him to call the law or something.

This was a town in which everyone knew everyone else, and most of their business. Melba's father, Red Curtis, was a well-thought-of farmer in the area, and he and Mr. Smelser were well acquainted. I was soon to learn that the banker liked and respected Melba, and that he had no compunction about looking after her best interests. The term *uptight* was just coming into vogue then, and that's what I was. To some, my lifelong dedication to alertness and attention to detail might be construed as nothing more than having shifty eyes, and believe me,

I'd been looking things over from the moment we walked in. Mr. Smelser didn't know what I was there for, but he sensed something. If I could have faded into the woodwork, I would've done it.

After they greeted each other and got the small talk out of the way, Melba introduced me to the characteristically stodgy bank president. Thrift was laced through his dark suit like shingles on a roof. He was a consummate example of his profession. If this had been a movie starring the Marx Brothers, Three Stooges, or Abbott and Costello, Mr. Smelser would have played the part of the banker.

He managed a tight smile as we shook hands, then he motioned toward the two chairs in front of his desk. After we took our seats, Melba told him she needed to borrow three hundred dollars, not giving any indication of what its intended use might be. All the while, the banker hardly took his eyes off me. Melba had a steady job and was an excellent candidate for a bank loan, but he was cautious.

"And what do you do, Tom? . . . Oh, you're in the air force . . . and you sell vacuum cleaners . . . hmm . . . I see."

"Yes, sir, and shoes on the side."

"Shoes . . . yes, well . . . Melba, are you sure you want to do this?" he asked, his neck almost snapping as he turned to her. "Three hundred dollars is a lot of money."

By this time, I was beginning to squirm, but Melba was as cool and pretty as a day in May.

"Yes, I'm sure, Mr. Smelser," she said, smiling confidently.

I can imagine now what that banker was thinking as he stared holes through me. But he had known the Curtis family for generations, and being aware that Melba was from such excellent lineage, he decided to OK the loan.

When we walked out of there a little while later, we were on our way to having our own set of wheels again. With that three hundred dollars, there was enough to pay three past-due car notes of eighty-six dollars each, along with a portion of another one looming on the horizon.

"I hate this," I told her on the way back to Altus. "I'll pay it back if it's the last thing I do." There usually wasn't a sincere bone in my body, but this time, I meant it.

"I know you will, and it *won't* be the last thing you do." She reassured me with that knowing smile.

I could get used to that kind of attitude, I thought to myself. *I can't let this one get away.* I might not have been the smartest guy in the world, but I could work circles around anybody, so I figured I could get by in life. But with a helpmate like her, the sky would be the limit.

From that day on, Melba and I were on the same wavelength, sharing a bond of understanding that made me feel as if we'd known one another forever. And we did pay off that loan. She had signed a twelve-month note, but I got busy selling vacuum cleaners and paid it off in six. Today, if I bring up the subject and ask her if I ever paid off that loan, she always smiles and says, "No, and you never will."

As we grew to know each other there in Oklahoma, I had never felt so close, so comfortable with anyone. After work each day, and on the occasional day off, we began to spend every waking moment together. Some bitter memories were still fresh—memories I wanted to forget, and never planned to talk about with anyone. But I never could keep anything to myself, and Melba and I had grown so close so quickly that after only a few weeks together, I began to blurt it all out to her. I had done my best to keep up a cheerful front, but she sensed that I was still suffering from some kind of unhealed wound. I know she was shocked to hear that I had been married—and *stunned* to learn that I had two children. Nice girls just didn't get hooked up with guys like me, and Melba was a *nice* girl. I had dreaded telling her about the marriage and the children because I was afraid that would be the last straw and our relationship would be over. Yet I knew I had to do it, and when I did, Melba showed only tenderness and compassion, sharing the pain I was feeling. She never exhibited a trace of the hurt I must have been causing her by confiding the truth in the only way I knew how: coarsely and abruptly.

I'd heard of *real* love, *true* love, and I was now experiencing it for the first time, rebound or no rebound. I found myself telling her my deepest, darkest secrets. I had no choice. I had never trusted anyone so much. I had a feeling she already knew something about my situation and because of a few early incidents was quickly zeroing in on the problem. Now and then, we'd be heading somewhere, and I would miss a certain turn, even with its name as plain as day. "Didn't you see that sign?" she would ask casually. Things like that must have told her something, along with the fact that I totally ignored menus in restaurants.

"Got it memorized," I said with a smile when one was offered. Then I'd pray that they served whatever I happened to order.

I grew tired of trying to fake it with her, and I actually began feeling I was being dishonest about it where she was concerned. Fancy that.

Finally, I just blurted it out one night. To celebrate the sale of a vacuum cleaner, we'd gone to a nice restaurant for dinner, and I ordered my usual hamburger.

"Tom," she said, "you always order hamburgers. Why don't you try something new for a change?" She pointed down to the menu in front of her. "Here, look at this choice of great dishes."

Just my luck, I thought, glancing down. Not a single picture I could point to on the page. Instead, it was filled with a lot of words I didn't know.

"Melba, I can't read," I said, looking straight into her eyes. There—it was done, and I felt relief already. "I order hamburgers because I can't read the menu."

I searched her face for a response. At first, she thought I was teasing her, as usual, because she started to smile. But then she realized I was serious. She didn't say anything for what seemed like forever.

"I don't believe you," she exclaimed finally.

"It's true," I said, then said it again with conviction. "It really is."

She stared at me in disbelief for a long time, studying my face. At last, she said, "So . . . you'll learn!"

Sometimes, Melba could be so frustratingly matter-of-fact.

At that point, I think we were both relieved. She had known *something* was wrong, and as maniacal as I could be sometimes, my being illiterate would have been the least of her fears. It appeared not to bother her at all. Her attitude was, "OK, so what? Let's make it work."

Of course, Melba could see how deeply ashamed I was of my illiteracy and did all she could to lessen my embarrassment. Certainly she was concerned, not only with my situation, but also with my feelings, so she took care of the immediate problem first with light banter and laughter, pumping optimism and enthusiasm back into my deflated ego.

We had been dating for a few months when I mustered out of the service and went to work full-time as a door-to-door vacuum cleaner salesman for Casey Southern. I'd been moonlighting six nights or more a week for Casey while I was still in the air force, but my hours were even longer now than when I had been trying to hold down two jobs. I began trudging from door to door for as many as twelve to fourteen hours a day, taking my unfinished paperwork with me to Melba's apartment in Altus and spreading it out on her dining table. Calmly and methodically, she would help me.

Then, so that we could be closer together, she transferred to a similar job in Lawton. I was working so hard to keep up with the others, but dozens of sales were being lost because I couldn't write up the orders. I found myself working late almost every night in a struggle to fulfill my self-imposed quotas. Discouraged and angry with myself, for diversion I began stopping off at the tavern to flirt with the waitresses and shoot a game or two of pool with the other salesmen. I was so good at it that I often wound up winning more money at the table than I'd earned all day peddling vacuum cleaners. But if flirting was nothing more than inappropriate, shooting pool was considered a lowlife pastime in those days, and I couldn't convince Melba it was a respectable way to generate a second income. We wound up arguing about it all the time, and finally she'd had enough.

"I'm not going to go on living like this," Melba told me one night when I dropped by with a pocketful of winnings. "We've been going out together almost a year now, and you're not treating me right. You're out playing pool every night, coming by with beer on your breath, and no telling what else. That's no way to live and it's no way to earn a living, and you know it. I want a husband and a family and a nice little house and a white picket fence and a dog and a cat. If you're not ready for that—if you're not ready to settle down and commit yourself to a life together—then we may as well close up shop now and move on. I have other things to do and places to go, and that means I will immediately begin dating other people."

Whew! I stood there and listened as solemnly as possible to every word she uttered. But I was the one who was supposed to talk like that and issue ultimatums, and here I was taking it from a woman. I knew the guy she was talking about too. Someone from New Mexico that I'd found out about. Or Melba's boss, a captain. He'd been trying to date her, and I didn't like him a bit. He wasn't even an enlisted man.

It was a sermon, all right, and Melba had a delivery that made it a powerful one. Now I don't like disruptions, never did. They always threw me off track, upset my sometimes delicate constitution, and spoiled my concentration, and here I was *caus-*

ing a disruption. But I wasn't about to mess up this deal. I had to put the quietus on this before it went any farther. So I decided to put a little reverse English on the situation.

"Honey, I love you with all my heart. But I don't deserve you. I'm not a good catch. I'm not even what you'd call a good *guy*. I'm only twenty-one, and I've already made a mess of my life. I'm just a dummy, and I don't know how I'm ever going to amount to anything. Why would you want to be married to somebody like *me*?"

By this time, I was squeezing tears from my eyes, but I realized that I wasn't just fishing around for favors and forgiveness—I was *meaning* everything I said.

"Darn it, Tom! There isn't anybody like you!" Melba said angrily, but with compassion. "That's what I like about you. Not just who you are, but who you're going to be. Look how much you've managed to accomplish without even knowing how to read. Just think what you could do if you learned to read. You're so smart and so bright and informed—about everything. And you've got the drive and the stamina and the desire to succeed. You just need to be more disciplined in your thinking and in your doing. But most of all, you need to believe in yourself! You can learn to read, and you will. There isn't anything you can't do if you make up your mind to do it. That's how much faith I've got in you! The question is, how much faith do you have in yourself?"

I couldn't answer. I knew by now that I couldn't do it without her, but she definitely did not need me. She could make it fine without this jerk. Was I going to be a victim, feel sorry for myself, make excuses for my mistakes, blame God or fate for my sorry plight, or was I going to knuckle down and take responsibility for my life?

I'd like to say that I turned it all around that day and we lived happily forever after, but I guess I really was a slow learner. For the next few months, I worked harder than ever to make a go of it as a vacuum cleaner salesman, and on weekends when I saw her, Melba pitched in like a trooper to complete the orders I couldn't fill out myself. My income began to improve, and for the most part, I even cleaned up my act after hours.

Melba and I had been dating for several months and had confided in each other our innermost thoughts, dreams, and fears. We were in tune on almost everything. There was no doubt that this was the person I wanted to spend the rest of my life with. All the elements were present. But all the members of Melba's family didn't share our enthusiasm. One of her sisters was skeptical. She wasn't sure I could be trusted and thought I might not be as loyal to Melba as I should be. Melba kept trying to assure her sister that she just didn't know me well enough and she would soon see. But I was still a young man overflowing in copious sociability, coupled with an unmatched exuberance for life, and one night I found Melba in tears when I arrived at her apartment. I asked what was wrong, and she said that her sister had come by for a visit that afternoon. Her sister got right to the point. While running errands during her lunch break, she had seen me in my car with another girl, and it sure didn't look like business.

"You can do better than Tom," her sister had insisted, and, of course, she probably would've liked to see Melba dating that captain.

Melba tells me now that she wondered why her sister and others couldn't see the same person she saw when she looked at me. "Why couldn't they see his potential—his ideals, his hopes and dreams, his vision, his zeal to get on with life, and his passion to become somebody—a person of value? Sometimes, after those sessions with my sister, doubts would creep into my mind. Was I so blinded by his charisma, his optimism, and his fun side that I was failing to see his faults? Was I out of my mind?"

Melba hadn't said a word to me up to that moment, but she

admitted it wasn't the first time her family and friends had expressed doubts about my character and my prospects. When she had reaffirmed her faith in me and her love for me as usual, she said her sister protested, "If he loves you so much, where's the ring?" She told me I had been sidestepping the issue every time she raised the subject of marriage, and she was beginning to have second thoughts about committing herself to me. "Maybe I'm making a terrible mistake," she said to me through her tears.

Well, at that a shiver of dread and fear went through me. It was like an electric shock. I'd never been as frustrated, never been as confused over a woman. I'd never allowed myself to be concerned about what anybody thought of my lifestyle, never worried about what time I was getting home, or what would be said. The fact was, I'd never been in love so deeply, and now, because of some juvenile flirtation that had meant nothing, she had me red-handed.

"OK, you're right," I told Melba. "But if you'll forgive me, I'd like to ask—Would you marry me?"

She looked at me, and I knew that if I wasn't committing right then and there, this very day, it was all over.

"You've got to make some changes in your behavior."

I told her I would. I don't think she really ever did say yes. She just started laughing and crying at the same time and threw her arms around me. I guess that was a "Yes."

"Doubts about Tom would overwhelm my thoughts until my head was spinning," Melba says now. "Then Tom would appear with that confident smile and those doubts washed away as if they had never been there. I don't know how I knew that he had that something special, but I did. And when you know you're right, just do it!"

And we did. The next day I put down twenty dollars I couldn't afford on an engagement ring.

Before I even had a chance to think about it, the wheels were set in motion. The little country church where Melba grew up was the chosen place, a date was set, flowers and a cake were ordered, and invitations were sent out. As each passing day was crossed off the calendar, I'm ashamed to say that I began to feel like a condemned man waiting for the day of execution. I didn't trust women, not any woman, and at that point I didn't even want to trust Melba.

She can't be that perfect, I would think to myself, knowing she could be, and was. *There has to be something wrong with her, and I won't find out what until it's too late to turn back,* I thought, knowing down deep that there was nothing wrong. At the same time, I still couldn't understand at all her reasons for sticking with me, knowing everything she knew. It just was beyond me.

Oh, there had been many ups and downs during our first year of getting to know each other, which was pretty normal, I guess. But recently there seemed to be more downs than ups. My silence and sense of dread began to cast a long shadow over Melba's own feelings again. The last few days before anyone's wedding are always stressful—the never-ending decisions to make and final preparations to complete. But I was pulling in the opposite direction, making it doubly hard on her.

The big day finally arrived—September 25, 1958—and I'll never forget the fifty-mile drive from Lawton to the church. All the way there, I was thinking up all kinds of reasons for getting mad and not going through with the wedding. I'd washed and polished that Plymouth till it looked like a Chrysler. I'd gotten myself a fresh haircut before getting all spiffed up in a dark suit, white shirt, and tie, then shined my new shoes until I could see my reflection in them. I was always a sharp dresser, and clean. If not a clean fighter, I've always been a clean person.

The highway from Lawton to Altus was smooth sailing that afternoon, but when I turned off for the drive to the church in the Consolidated Eight school system, where Melba had graduated at the top of her class and spent her starring days as a basketball player, the road turned into several miles of red Oklahoma dirt. The powdery dust settled over the outside of that pure white car and turned it orange. Inside, a film of dust covered the seats. All the other guests in the wedding party were gathering from every corner of the map, and my life was unfolding before my eyes as they passed me en route to the ceremony. If I'd been driving any slower, I would've been going backward. When Casey and Marie Southern went by, I could hear Marie talking about me through the open windows. I even saw Casey's brake lights come on as he peered through the rearview mirror. He almost stopped to see if anything was wrong, then I guess he understood and chuckled to himself. After they got out of sight, best man Johnny Earl Gaskel went by, and my foot backed off the accelerator a little more. It was a real toss-up there near the end of the trip. If the church had been another hundred yards down the road, I probably would have floored the Plymouth and kept on going. But suddenly I ran out of road and drove into the churchyard. There wasn't a house within ten miles.

Everybody was impatiently standing around inside the church when I finally arrived more than half an hour late, stepping out into that crusted-over clay and messing up my nice shine. One last time, I thought about getting back into the car and beating a hasty retreat. My head said go, but something tugged at my heart to stay.

Some of the guests were muttering impatiently as I walked through the door, and there was Johnny Earl grinning from ear to ear, and maid of honor Janny, who had grown up right here in this farming area with Melba. She and Lucky had just gotten married, and I was still hanging on to thoughts of freedom and thinking, *Hmm, if he hadn't let Janny introduce us, I wouldn't be about to walk down this aisle.*

But when I caught sight of Melba with love shining from her eyes, in her white wedding dress, waiting for me at the other end of the aisle in that little white meetinghouse known as the Community Friends Church, all the doubts and misgivings simply melted away. I knew with absolute certainty that everything was going to be all right. It was like a dream. So help me God, I saw this glow around her. This was where I belonged. This was the woman I was meant to share my life with. My soul mate.

The beginning of a beautiful marriage
I think Melba was as relieved as I look in this shot—
she just hid it better.

❖❖❖❖❖❖❖❖❖❖❖❖❖❖❖❖❖❖❖❖❖❖❖❖❖

As I passed the front pew to stand beside her, she saw it all in my eyes, and I felt the full impact of her love filling me with a strength and a joy I'd never felt before. I hoped my love was having the same effect. We exchanged vows without looking away from each other for a single moment, and when the pastor, Valentine Bridenstine—that's his *real* name—pronounced us man and wife, tears flowed down both our cheeks as we walked hand in hand back down the aisle to music played on the piano by the pastor's wife.

"Honey," I said to her as we walked out the front door into the bright sunshine and prepared to drive away to the Ozark Lodge at Lake Altus, "I know this has been said a million times, but I want you to come and ride the wave with me. We're going to make it in this world because I have you, and together we can do anything. The past doesn't matter, just the future, and nothing can stop us. Look out, life! Tom and Melba Harken are coming through to make it happen."

6

Making It Happen

*Me (second from back right) and one of my
early sales crews*

❖❖❖❖❖❖❖❖❖❖❖❖❖❖❖❖❖❖❖❖❖❖❖

ξ·I meant every word of my vow to Melba. But it's just as well
I had no idea what a bumpy ride it would be on that wave
together. I might've sunk without a trace long ago. And if she'd
known, she might have bailed out in search of life on a more
even keel. But she stayed with me, and the only reason I didn't
give up, the only reason I'm still alive, the only reason I've managed to amount to a hill of beans, is the fact that she *didn't* give
up on me. Melba was the only one who knew me for what I was
and somehow loved me anyway. God knows why.

In the weeks before and after the wedding, I had knocked
myself out competing in a vacuum cleaner sales contest. The
prize was a trip to Cleveland, Ohio, home of the Scott and
Fetzer Company who manufactured Kirby, along with other
quality appliances. Casey told me I was close to winning the

contest, so we postponed the honeymoon for a few days just in case. Got married on a Saturday, and Monday morning I was knocking on doors again. Well, I won, and believe me, Cleveland was the big time for two hicks from the sticks.

Even getting there was fun. It proved to be our first plane ride together—Melba's first anywhere—and from the time we touched down, we were walking on air. It was red carpet all the way. They even gave us tip money, had all bases covered. I love a company like that. Melba had never seen a building over four stories high, and we craned our necks looking up at the skyscrapers. At one point we were given a grand tour of the Kirby factory, introduced to all the executives, and even met the man who invented the Kirby vacuum cleaner back in 1906, Mr. James B. Kirby.

Members of the Cleveland Browns attended the big banquet and joined us at our tables. Boy, were we excited! That would be like having dinner today with the Dallas Cowboys. We hardly knew what to *say*. And all those four- and five-course meals served with wine. Wow—another first! New York City couldn't have been more impressive.

After the honeymoon and all the festivities had ended, we returned to our jobs, secure in the thought that we were going to live happily ever after. Our dreams were coming true, and we were embarking on the really important phase of our life together—the part about a guy and a girl always being together through thick and thin—sharing and caring and loving. What more could a man ask, I told myself, than the love of a good woman and a job he enjoys.

Dean Jeffers, a dear friend and a master in the selling field for many years, once passed along some philosophic thoughts about salesmen. The respected chairman emeritus of Nationwide Insurance Company wrote to me in a letter, "What I like about salesmen is they get much more out of life because they put so much more into it." Wow! And it's still true!

Any born salesman will tell you he loves his job, and I'm no exception. Salesmen seem to have more energy and zest than other groups. They're always moving, always in the thick of things. I love all aspects of selling—the challenge, the approach, the wheeling and dealing, and finally, the ultimate high, closing the deal. That's what I'm thinking of when I tell employees, "Go out there and make it happen." Salesmen get up with that—and go to bed with it.

Being a married man now, I knew I was going to need to double up on making *something* happen, so before long I was working even longer hours than before. The honeymoon definitely wasn't over—it still isn't—but we people tend to wake up fast when reality is standing at the windows peering in. That may be where the term *mover and shaker* originated, I don't know, but I do know I was out there knocking on a hundred doors a day before anyone would agree to a demonstration, let alone a sale, and most nights I wouldn't get home until around eleven or twelve. And more often than not, the number of Kirby vacuum cleaners owned by the population hadn't increased in Lawton, Oklahoma.

Melba was forever waiting up for me, always there with a hug and a kiss and a word of encouragement. Yet I seemed never to take home enough money for us to get by on, and I wanted desperately to support my wife. That's just the way it was, and it meant a lot to me to reach the point where I could actually make the grade. The more I thought of it, the more it burned into my mind. We were living, but we weren't living well, and I wanted to give Melba all the finer things in life. The term *shame* isn't used much anymore because many have come to accept just about anything as the norm. But back then, if you didn't measure up to your own standards, you were expected to feel ashamed of yourself. And I did. I felt like a failure. I felt unworthy of Melba.

But she wasn't really worried. Her income paid for at least

half of the expenses, and I was sure I'd be able to cover the rest. She was also confident that together we could solve any problem we might face. So she set about making a home for us. Miss Melba found a little two-bedroom duplex apartment that was just perfect. It was located halfway between my Kirby office and her office at Fort Sill. It was on the corner across the street from an elementary school that had a tennis court where we could go on Sunday afternoons to hit a few balls. We were the perfect couple—Melba could do the housekeeping and the bookkeeping, and I could go out and make us a fortune.

Pressures grew, and frustration built along with the pressure. I had stopped hanging out with the boys in the weeks before and since the wedding, but I started missing their company again. Melba was an uncommonly intelligent, beautiful, and classy lady. My male friends were anything but. These guys were common, and I guess my subconscious was seeking its own level. Besides, at the end of long days and evenings of slammed doors, I would be feeling so guilty and angry with myself that I couldn't face the thought of going home to my wife empty-handed. So I started taking the long way home again and stopping off at the tavern for a few games of pool and a couple of beers with the other salesmen. For an hour or so, it would take the edge off my frustration. But by the time I let myself in the front door around two or three in the morning, I'd know what was coming: a scene so excruciating I would wish I hadn't come home at all.

After sitting all night in the window of our darkened house, Melba would look at me in pain as I walked in the door. I'd pretend to be sober, have a silly smile, and want a hug as though everything was normal—like I was just coming home from work. Melba would get so angry, but usually she just held her tongue and glared at me—shaking her head in bewilderment with a look on her face that said, "When are you ever going to just grow up?"

Years later, she would tell me how relieved she was when she heard the car pull into the drive, but she'd be so hurt that she, too, would almost be wishing I hadn't come home at all. I can't blame her. I would have a chip on my shoulder and, without anybody else to take it out on, I'd take it out verbally on Melba, the only one I truly loved. I would never have harmed her physically, but in helpless rage and futility, my uneducated voice packed a wallop that hurt even worse. And I was good at choosing just the right word that I knew would hurt the most.

No matter what she said to me when I finally got home, it would never be the right thing, and if I could make her mad enough to fly off the handle, I wouldn't have to feel so guilty. The tears hurt even more than the anger, but both were unbearable—for Melba and me. We weren't the kind of people who fought all the time, we both knew that, and we had the same dreams and ambitions. What neither of us realized was that my illiteracy was pulling a part of me in the opposite direction. I wanted it not to matter that I couldn't read or write, but every day I spent out there facing a world filled with what I saw as educated people, it mattered big-time.

These confrontations between the two of us turned into such grim rituals that I found myself spending even more time on the road every night and stopping off to kill time shooting pool and preserving my immaturity, so that I could postpone the hour I'd have to go home and face reality. Even after Melba became pregnant a few months later, I wouldn't go home at night to spend more time with her. I was so obsessed with work, so intent on trying to pay the bills, that I buried myself in selling and training other salesmen to sell. That was my pitiful, empty little world, and being home alone most of the time was hers.

How fitting that I was in a business dominated by the word *vacuum*. I was *living* in one. If most men lead lives of quiet desperation, illiterate people lead lives of *screaming frustration*. We must have purpose in our lives, a reason to get up in the morning, something to kick us in the backside and make us want to *go*. But it seemed I was spending most of the time kicking myself, and not getting anywhere. To me, somehow it was all God's fault, and I was mad at Him. How easy it is to focus accusations, when we know we have only ourselves to blame for most of our problems.

Just as the blind and the deaf can let themselves sink into a morass of darkness and silence, an illiterate with no self-respect and no direction in his life can sink into hopelessness and withdraw to the point of disappearing. Thank God I didn't do that, but neither did I pay enough attention to what was happening with Melba, not even on the night she went into labor with our first son. Oh, I made a big point of driving her to the hospital. I even stayed with her for a while, but the moment they admitted her, I started feeling jittery about sitting there in that waiting room.

Miss Melba and Tommy Jr.

Then my worst fear was realized. Someone from the hospital staff came up to me in the waiting room and wanted me to fill out papers to admit Melba. The old terror gripped me as surely as if I'd been back in that schoolroom with my palms sweating, so shook up I couldn't spell *cat*. I couldn't do it. They were going to find out I couldn't read or write. I'd be a laughingstock. The whole hospital would know, the whole town, the whole world.

So I ran. Out of that waiting room and out of the hospital to the only place I'd been comfortable in for quite some time—the office. Once there I locked the door, left the lights off, sat at my desk, and stared into the darkness until my eyes burned, then filled with tears. Tears of fear, tears for Melba, tears for myself, but most of all, tears for a child who was about to enter the world and live with an illiterate father.

Next thing I knew, of course, it was morning, and Casey Southern was standing there telling me I had a son. I could tell he was disgusted with me, but not nearly as disgusted as I was with myself. I should have been there with her, holding her hand, grinning from ear to ear and handing out cigars or something. In that harsh dawn, I hurried to the hospital to see my wife and my new son, but I could tell I had hurt her worse than I ever had before. She put it behind us long ago, but I never could. After all these years, I still cringe when I think of it, and no excuse in the world would justify my inaction and insensibility.

Then I did something even more stupid. When Tommy Jr. was about six months old, Melba began awaking in the night with abdominal pains that kept getting worse and worse. I assumed it had something to do with having the baby. Since she was seeing the doctor about it, I figured she would soon be all right and I wouldn't have to worry about it. But it continued for the next couple of months, and she wasn't getting any better. I still didn't think there was anything for me to do about it, so I just kept working almost around the clock.

I was at the office one night when she called and said she

needed me to take her to the hospital. Like a complete jackass, I told her I was in the middle of an important training job and couldn't leave. She called her sister and told her to go by the office and insist that I go with them to the hospital. But I figured I had to set a good example in front of the other salesmen by showing them my dedication to the job. I was completely inflexible and flatly refused to leave my desk. I'll regret that until the day I die.

The doctors in the emergency room immediately admitted her to intensive care. Diagnosed with peritonitis, Melba almost died, and once again I wasn't there for her. She told me later how she came to understand why I can't seem to tolerate sickness in any form—it was because of the terrible experiences of my youth—but that doesn't excuse what I did, or rather didn't do. I even left it to Casey's wife, Marie, to take care of Tommy Jr. for the two weeks Melba stayed in the hospital. She even went back to work before she was absolutely well, and in addition to that, she was about to become a mother again.

Unbelievably enough, our low ebb was yet to come. It was about four months later, and I was keeping myself so busy that there was little time remaining to engage in customary pursuits of young marrieds. Nevertheless, we were expectant parents again. And I was still in shock about the birth of our *first* child. With the strain of three mouths to feed now, and ever-mounting hospital bills, our situation had become similar to my parents' during *my* long illness as a child. Bills aside, again I was the one at a distance, but this time for a different reason, if indeed there was any reasoning behind it. I was still spending most of my time away from home—either selling or at the office, or, yes, shooting pool. I was always making excuses, weak as they were. I can't even pin it on my young age. I was still in my early twenties, but that's old enough to know better.

I wasn't taking home enough money to feed one baby, let alone two. One morning as I left for work, I told Melba I didn't have enough money on me to pay for the can of condensed milk she needed to make formula for Tommy Jr. When I wandered back home around ten that night, she looked at me, then spoke very quietly and clearly. There was something in her tone that let me know this was it—the end of our marriage or the end of my juvenile behavior.

"The thirty-five cents you spent on beer or pool or whatever it was," she said very coolly, "would have bought a quart of milk for the baby."

That went through me like a knife. Instead, she had fed him sugar-water. I looked at her, and heard Tommy crying, then lowered my eyes and stared at the floor. I figured as long as my head was bowed I might as well say a prayer, so I mouthed silently, "God, this is me talking, and I want You to know . . . I'm not mad at You anymore. I just need Your help."

7

From Number One to Square One

Sales trophies were hard to come by in my door-to-door days, but they finally led me right into the Kirby Hall of Fame.

❖❖❖❖❖❖❖❖❖❖❖❖❖❖❖❖❖❖❖❖❖❖❖

What little free time I allowed myself was spent with Melba, and our relationship gradually improved. I was still an illiterate living with a valedictorian, but she didn't flaunt her intellect, and I tried not to show my ignorance.

The only thing I really knew about was vacuum cleaners, but I still wasn't having that much luck selling them, and I couldn't figure out why not. Melba always sent me off to work in the morning like a cheerleader and greeted me with a warm smile and words of encouragement when I got home at night. But when sales didn't improve over a period of several weeks, I began arriving at home more depressed and frustrated than ever. Finally one night she asked if it might have something to do with my sales technique: "Why don't you let me go on a few calls with you?"

Well, I swelled up like a toad at that impertinence. Selling was the one thing I could do half right, and here was my wife questioning my sales skills.

"What would you know about selling?" I snapped. But something definitely was wrong, so I let her talk me into it.

Next day, my first call was at the home of an air force lieutenant, and I wasn't looking forward to it. My military memories were unpleasant to begin with, and brass always made me feel so . . . unimportant. But I could fake anything, so with Melba at my side I put on a self-assured smile—she told me later it came across as snobbish—and rapped on the door. The second-louie and his wife, who lived in the same neighborhood as we did, greeted us warmly, and I began to feel as though I might get lucky and make a sale.

Then, at some point about halfway through my presentation, the officer interrupted my demonstration by deciding to show off his technical knowledge.

"What's the RPM of that machine?" he barked with the authority of a general and the tact of an oaf.

"What do you mean?" I asked, not quite connecting with his left-field question.

"How fast does the motor turn?"

I could have punched him, and probably would have if Melba hadn't been sitting there taking notes. I kept my voice level but couldn't resist throwing in a barb. "Tell you what, why don't I turn this baby on, and you can just *count* how fast that blade's turning."

I was pretty pleased with myself at that. But without another word he showed us out the door before the coffee got cold, and we were back on the street. The day was already over for me, and it wasn't even noon. I was prepared for a lecture from Melba, but certainly not the one I got the moment we got back in the car.

"OK, what'd I do wrong?" I growled, ready.

"Well, first of all, if I were the customer and you came to my front door with that nonchalant air, I wouldn't like you either."

"What do you mean?"

"Well, as soon as customers open the door, you're mad at them before you get inside, and they can feel it."

"Go on," I said, reluctantly beginning to understand, but not really wanting to hear it.

"I'm surprised you haven't spotted it before now," she said. "You need to change your attitude and become more likable. As bad as we need a sale, you act as though you don't care whether you sell a vacuum cleaner or not, and I wouldn't buy one from you either."

"You wouldn't?"

"Of course not," she said. "Not with the way you were behaving in there. We both know you feel inferior because you can't read or write, but you're as good as anyone else, and I know you're just as smart as anyone else, so you should start *acting* like it."

Lately, I had found myself *acting* most of the time. I felt as though my whole life was an act, and a bad one at that.

"What does that word mean?" I asked Melba.

"What does what word mean?"

"Inf . . . infar . . . you know."

"Inferior?"

"Yeah, that's it," I said with a smile, trying to lighten the moment with a touch of humor. "I thought it meant the inside of a house."

"Oh, Tom, you always make me laugh." Yes, we were poor as prodigal church mice, and always living on the edge, but as long as we could laugh, we would make it.

On the way home, instead of preaching about my volatile temper, Melba quietly reasoned with me, and a whole new realm of possibilities began to open. She was shedding light on things that never had occurred to me before.

With my winning and less-than-winning ways, I could always make people laugh, and I sure could make them cry whether I meant to or not, so why not push another button or two and make them *buy*?

Somewhere I'd heard about something called "power of purpose," about people supposedly *willing* things to happen by pure force of thought. I'd always been a rather forceful guy physically, so maybe that kind of strength could be channeled onto the mental side. There certainly was no overcrowding problem in my brain. Plenty of room for improvement up there.

Room for improvement. Those three words can open new worlds of possibility when your old world looks uninhabitable. We can always do something different today, do something constructive, something helpful, something kind. Even by performing the smallest of tasks, you can develop a sense of accomplishment, then build on that until you become a powerhouse in whatever arena you choose. My good friend Joe Dudley made it almost through high school before he realized one day that he'd missed something. That something was knowledge, and he made the decision to retrace his trail and find it. Along the way, Joe found himself.

It all started with that kick on the backside we call impetus, impulse, push, or motivation. Joe's compelling force was a girl he liked in school. One day she told Joe that she was breaking up with him to go with another guy, and she mentioned his name. "Why do you want to go with him?" Joe asked. "He's ugly, and I'm better looking than he is."

"You're dumb," she said. "He's smarter than you and can make me a better living than you could if we ever got married." As Joe says, that woke him up.

Today, Joe is the founder, president, and CEO of Dudley Products, Inc., one of the most successful businesses owned by an African American in the U.S. I've heard Joe tell his touching story several times, about how he was considered retarded, about the encouragement of his mother—but Joe wasn't so dumb. He started from scratch, going back to his first book in the first grade. Joe carefully went over every word in that book. It was fairly easy for him at this point. Then he moved on to his second-grade book. That wasn't so tough either. Then the third-grade. Might start getting a little difficult from here on. But no matter. Joe read and reread until he understood everything there was to understand, then moved on.

By the time Joe Dudley caught up with his class, he was a force to be reckoned with, and he had a new attitude. A winning attitude. Joe's situation wasn't so different from my own. Both of us stumbled and bumbled our way through the early years with losing attitudes, and the fact was, at the time we didn't care. We were like a 1950s trucker I knew who transported large loads in a broken-down vehicle. He infuriated other drivers with a sign on his back bumper reading, "I may be slow, but I'm ahead of *you*!" Joe and I shared a similar chip-on-the-shoulder disposition, but eventually we came to realize that in order to get by in this world, we must learn to care. That was a hard lesson, but once it sank in, we became different people.

Thanks to Melba's insightful advice, I began turning over new leaves like a whirling dervish. I could care even when I *didn't* care, when I didn't *have* to care, when there was no *need* to care. I became a caring guy. Instead of Tom-the-Atom-Bomb, I became *Reverend* Harken, at least in the part of the brain that rules the beast in all of us. And y'know, it *worked*!

On my very next house call, a middle-aged lady who had obviously gotten up on the wrong side of the world answered the knock, peeked out through a crack, and before I could even introduce myself, slammed the door in my face. *The heat must be getting to her*, I thought as I mopped the back of my neck with a handkerchief. No problem. Instead of losing my temper and kicking her dog, let alone giving up, I walked briskly around to the back door and knocked again. This time she frowned when she saw me, but paused as if trying to put together what had just happened. That was all the time I needed.

"Ma'am, I don't know if you're aware of it, but there's a mean old lady living in front of you, but you seem like a much nicer person than she is, and I'm hoping you'll give me the chance to speak to you for a few minutes."

She couldn't keep from smiling at that, and next thing you know I was sitting at her kitchen table having ice-cold lemonade and listening to her life story. When I walked out the front door two hours later with a check in my hand, there was a brand-new, deluxe-model Kirby vacuum cleaner sitting in her living room. And even if the car was old, a brand-new Tom Harken drove away in it.

It was amazing what I could accomplish with a little humility—and a lot of patience. Plus, I genuinely began to care about people and listen to people. And I think I was beginning to grow up. I still had to knock on a hundred doors in order to make three or four appointments, and maybe, just maybe, sell one vacuum cleaner. But I refused to become discouraged. Heck, we had to eat and pay the bills. I couldn't *afford* to become discouraged. I did whatever it took to get in the door, even reducing myself to getting down on my knees if necessary. Hey, desperate people do desperate things.

I'd say something like, "You look like a kind woman, so I know you'll understand when I tell you my company will pay me only if I give you a demonstration to show how wonderfully this remarkable vacuum cleaner works."

"Well, I don't know . . ." She would hesitate, giving me the once-over, hearing me out only because of her reluctance to tackle the load of laundry that was waiting for her.

"Please, lady, just give me a chance to earn a little bit of a living," I would pitch. "I promise to be out of your life forever if you'll just give me fifteen minutes of your time."

That usually did it, and once inside the door, I had to create that old salesman's standby: the want, need, and desire for the product. I had to divert her thoughts and lift them from housework and daily problems to new heights, new dreams, a new *vacuum cleaner*. Hopefully, she would and could buy, but nine times out of ten, the husband would have to be present to give the final OK. I very seldom sold a vacuum cleaner without returning later when both were there.

When I was selling door-to-door, it was a surprise to see a woman write a check. Women couldn't get credit to purchase houses, cars, or even smaller items. They were treated like second-class citizens, and it was only grudgingly that they had been allowed the vote not so many years earlier. Even if he was raised in a barn, the *man* of the house was the first and final word. And to be completely honest, even a worthless drunk got more respect in the community than a woman of immaculate reputation. Difficult to imagine today, but that's the terrible way it was as recently as the 1950s. I suppose it's not politically correct these days to say "You've come a long way, baby," but being from the old school and a child of the '40s, it's still a term of endearment to me. I hold all women in high regard, and treat them with utmost respect because they have had to struggle for every minor gain they've made over the years.

Thanks to some unsinkable pioneers, all that has changed. Melba is of course my number-one "pioneer," and I can call some of the others by name. The whole world owes thanks to such stars as the queen of cosmetics, Mary Kay Ash; Weight Watchers founder Dr. Jean Nidetch; porcelain potentate Helen Boehm, and many, many more. Miss Melba and I have had the privilege of meeting and becoming friends with these ladies who may seem delicate on the outside but are strong as steel on the inside. They've set the pace for women everywhere who wish to attain their highest goals, and the world owes them eternal thanks.

Selling to men required a different approach. They would usually turn me away if I didn't have an appointment with them. So I would try to make those arrangements during the daytime, returning in the evening when the husband was home. I knew he had to be there to give permission for the purchase, but I also knew he would be there under protest. After he's put in a hard day and kicked off his shoes, the last thing a husband wants to see is a door-to-door vacuum cleaner salesman who hopes to get into his pocket. In order to get his attention and hold it, I would quickly seat both of them close together on the couch, and then begin the presentation of all presentations. To show potential customers just how badly they needed a Kirby, I would substitute black squares of cloth for the vacuum cleaner bag and would vacuum around the couple, replacing the black cloth at regular intervals. With eight or ten of those cloths surrounding them, piled high with dirt, they were faced with dirt everywhere they went in the room. I could make them want the vac, and desire the vac. This made it obvious they now *needed* it. There was such a mountain of dirt piled up, they wouldn't be able to walk over it and get to the bedroom that night until I made it disappear for them.

The machine would suck it all up in no time, and while they were still recovering from this miracle, I would resort to a sure-fire routine that closed hundreds of deals for me: "That's a pretty dramatic demonstration, isn't it?" I'd tell them, looking back and forth with deep sincerity, first to her, then to him. "This should show you more effectively than anything I might say that there isn't a finer vacuum cleaner in the world. But do you really need the best? Well, Mary and John, do you remember how you felt about each other when you first got married? John, you could hardly wait to move into your new home and begin your life together. You wanted nothing but the best for

Mary, and that includes the best vacuum cleaner money can buy, just like the one you would have bought for her if you'd had the chance to purchase a Kirby for her then. Well, tell me something, John. Do you love your wife as much today as you did when you asked her to marry you?"

That was the clincher. Worked almost every time. I'd reach out to shake his hand and tell him, "John, let's let her have it, what do you say?"

Well, I had him in a corner. He couldn't say no. If he did, he'd be facing some chilly nights no matter the time of year. I'd whip out that sales contract and get his signature on the dotted line. I was excellent with figures, always had been. I knew when I'd earned ten or fifty dollars, or whatever. I just couldn't read words. Only when people bought my products on credit did I have any problems. Relying on my well-honed memory to get all the information needed for processing the papers, how long had they lived at this address, did they rent or own, where did he work, and for how long, where else had they established credit, and things like that. Since I couldn't read or write, I sometimes would ask the lady of the house to fill out the credit application while I bided time showing various attachments to the husband. But if this was not possible, I'd memorize all these details, then pack up my gear—and the signed contract—and make tracks out of there. The deal had to be closed that night. I had created the want, need, and desire, and if I left without getting the money, they could go buy a cheaper one at Sears the next morning. By the time I left a home, it might be ten or eleven at night, but Melba would be waiting for me with a kiss and asking how it went. While the details were still fresh, I would relate to her all the facts, names, addresses, whatever, and she'd write up the order for me.

My sales started picking up so fast that within a month I was Casey's number-one salesman. That's when the trouble started: He promoted me to sales manager. If I do say so myself, I was a pretty good salesman by then, and I just *knew* I was cut out to be a leader. But on some level, I resented the other salesmen for not doing better than they were, despite the fact that they could read and write. I was cocky and intolerant. Demanding not only the same efforts but also the same results, I drove the other salesmen as hard as I was driving myself. I expected them to work as hard as I worked, and to have that burning desire to get ahead in life. Morale among the staff began falling like a stone, and so did sales.

*In front of Casey Southern, I sign a contract making me a
factory distributor for Kirby and moving Melba and me to Texas.*

❖❖❖❖❖❖❖❖❖❖❖❖❖❖❖❖❖❖❖❖❖❖❖❖❖❖❖❖❖

Casey's patience was wearing thin, and that didn't bode well for me.

"Tom, you're having a lot of trouble with your salesmen, and with yourself," he said to me one day. "Something isn't clicking, so I'm going out with you this morning, and we're going to knock on doors—you'll take one side of the street, and I'll take the other—and we're going to find out what it is."

Well, that shook me up. Casey had eyes in the back of his head. He could read people better than anyone I ever met, and he was reading me well. Here was the master about to put a kid through his paces, and I certainly wasn't looking forward to it. Casey could be very intimidating when he wanted to be, and that made matters worse. I was stuttering before we got to the car.

We selected a likely Lawton neighborhood, and sure as the world, just as I parked the car a tire went flat. Not wanting to reveal any inadequacy, I promptly began fixing the flat.

"Don't waste your time doing that," Casey said. "We'll call somebody to do it."

Uneasy, thinking this might be some kind of test, I just kept twisting on those lug nuts. Exasperated, Casey stalked off to a nearby house and knocked on the door. Twenty minutes later, he returned with a cash sale and a sixty-dollar commission— from *my* side of the street.

"Did you learn anything from that?" he asked. "It would've cost maybe three dollars to get that flat fixed, but you lost a sale and got greasy to boot."

I've never fixed a flat since. It was an important lesson—but I was still pushing my salesmen too hard.

The last straw for Casey came when I started docking pay when one arrived even a few minutes late for work—and I fired them after a second infraction. Oh, I was a pill, all right— maybe even a bad dose of medicine.

"Tell me something, Tom," Casey said one day. "How many vacuum cleaners do we have to sell around here to make a profit every month?"

"A hundred, Boss," I told him confidently.

"With our sales force, that's ten vacuum cleaners per salesman, isn't it, Tom?"

"That's about right, sir."

"Do you think you could sell that many all by yourself?"

"No way."

"Well, that must be what you have in mind, because you've fired the entire staff."

He had a point. "Don't worry, Casey," I said. "I'll step up productivity, and we'll bring in new people to make up for the slackers."

"We sure will, Tom, so I'm not worried about it," he said. "But as long as we're firing salesmen, let's make it unanimous. You're fired too."

I was enraged. Who did Casey think he was getting rid of *me*, his most gifted and productive salesman! I would teach him a lesson he'd never forget. Walking out the door, I went down the street and rented the first vacant office. I would open up my own vacuum cleaner distributorship, rehire all the salesmen I fired, and make him sorry he'd ever entered the vacuum cleaner business.

It took only four months to find out how wrong I was.

With hardly a sale in that time, we were depending almost entirely on the ninety bucks every other week from Melba's civil service job, which wasn't nearly enough to live on now that we had young Mark in addition to Tommy. We were way behind on the rent, utilities, and car payments. Melba was about at the end of her rope, and desperation drove her to call Casey's wife, Marie, who had been Melba's friend and confidante for some time. She implored Marie to arrange a meeting so that Casey and I could patch things up. I found out later it took Marie a month to talk him into it, and even though we were about to starve, I didn't like the idea one little bit.

"We've got an appointment to sit down with Casey and Marie," Melba said, broaching the subject one day.

"What for?" I demanded to know.

"To get you two talking again, Tom," she said. "We have to do something."

"Aw, I'll have it going my way in a couple more months," I told her, not at all sure of what I was saying.

"No," she said. "If you have to get on your hands and knees to ask him to take you back, then that's what you're going to do."

"No, I'm not!" I shouted.

"Yes, you are," Melba said, not even raising her voice, leaving the "or else" unsaid.

Ultimatums—I hate 'em, and normally I would've done just the opposite of whatever I was told to do, but that indication of "or else" sounded final. Besides, she was right. So, reluctantly, I went along with it and showed up with Melba for the meeting at Casey's home.

It was summertime, but there was definitely a chill in the air as formalities were dispensed with almost immediately. While Melba and Marie took down cups for coffee, Casey made it plain with his silence that he was in no mood to let me off the hook. He was waiting for me to do the talking, and I'd better tell a good story. I couldn't blame him, but that didn't make it any easier to stand there and listen to the indictment before the sentence was passed. I had to convince the master of all salesmen that I had learned my lesson and was ready to learn more. Eventually I sold the crusty old salesman, but he still wanted me to pay the price.

"You've done your best to ruin me since the day I fired you, and I won't ever forgive you for that," Casey said with all the fury of an apostolic preacher. "But for the sake of your wife and children, I'll give you one last chance to redeem yourself. Not here in Lawton, though. I don't want to be in the same town with you right now. But I'll let you try your luck in Elk City. If you can make it there, we'll see about exploring other possibilities."

I knew exactly what he was doing to me, but it was the only chance I was going to get. Elk City was a pleasant little town northwest of Lawton. Problem was, it was a *hundred miles* northwest of Lawton, and I started commuting both ways every day, returning late at night, often without earning enough to pay for the gas it took to get there and back. I seldom sold more than a few vacuum cleaner bags, belts, or brushes.

I remember one night, after leaving home without eating that morning, I finished my rounds about eight at night with exactly a dollar in my pocket. I had done two or three demonstrations that day with no luck. Vacuum cleaner belts were three for a dollar.

That dollar wasn't enough to pay for my dinner, much less the rest of the family. That's when I saw a sign above a ramshackle little drive-through joint offering three hamburgers for a dollar. Golly, those burgers smelled good! Giving my order to the carhop, I wondered if she could hear my stomach rumbling.

"That'll be $1.02, with tax," she said as she returned with the bag of burgers on her tray.

"But all I've got is a dollar," I said to her, a bit stunned.

"Well, you can't have these burgers unless you give me a dollar and two cents," she said.

"I don't have two cents," I told her. "All I've got is a dollar."

Turning around without another word, she took those hamburgers and went back inside. I drove all the way home that night with no food.

Maybe I could have scrounged around in the floor of the car or the glove compartment and found that two cents. I probably could have even turned on the charm and sweet-talked her into "loaning" it to me. I still had the dollar, so I could have stopped somewhere else for pork-and-beans and a loaf of bread. I don't know why I didn't, but it must have had something to do with the feeling of being totally beaten down and on the verge of giving up. That feeling is something between shell shock and T. S. Eliot's "ragged claws scuttling across the floor of darkened seas." I've seen others experience it many times over the years, and to this day I believe it's the memory of that one night that causes me to reach out and try to help and encourage poor souls who have that *look* about them—the look of defeat. One little boost can help so much.

At home later, Melba had made sure the boys were fed and

asleep, and then she prepared something for me. It's almost magical how women can make a meal out of virtually anything. When she realized how low I really felt, she gave me a hug and said, "You've just had a hard day, honey. We're going to be all right."

I wasn't too sure about that. In my whole life, I'd never felt like such a failure, and as I lay awake that night, I decided to do whatever it took from then on to straighten up my life and do better for all of us. Poverty wasn't for me. I'd had enough of it!

I kept plugging away every day, and we went on struggling—without a word of complaint. After six months, Casey finally felt I'd learned my lesson and brought me back to home base—and square one. I began all over again as a member of his ten-man sales staff, no different from a new recruit, except I knew where the rest room was, and where lots of my good intentions were buried. This time, things were different. I had paid my dues, and my sales were never better. Although I wasn't spending any more time at home than before, this time I was supporting Melba the way she'd always been there for me. I was finally beginning to give her the love, respect, and admiration she'd always deserved. I actually felt good about the life I was leading, for once no longer so consumed with ambition that I couldn't be happy with what I was doing—or at least a little bit more patient about it.

Without realizing it, I had learned one of the great lessons life has to teach.

8

Beaumont, Texas

Me as the young entrepreneur in my own building and my chosen city—Beaumont

❖❖❖❖❖❖❖❖❖❖❖❖❖❖❖❖❖❖❖❖❖❖❖❖❖

❖When you're not really looking for it—that's when fortune truly smiles. Within another six months, Casey offered me an opportunity to move up in the world as a Kirby area distributor in Altus, Oklahoma, a good-sized town about a hundred miles from Lawton in the opposite direction.

Our only drawback was the funds we'd need for stock, which I knew would be necessary and which I didn't have. "You'll have to have about five hundred dollars worth of merchandise," said Casey. "Can you handle that?"

"No problem," I said confidently, not having the slightest idea where I'd come up with it. Naturally, I didn't want to ask *him* for it. Remember, I was on the rebound with Casey, and lucky to still be on his payroll. So I went home and told Miss Melba about his proposition and our need for money. Our two neighbors were people of means, she said. Maybe we could ask them for a loan. This was another second lieutenant and his wife. He was one of the good ones. They lived in the duplex next door to us in Lawton and were young like us, but their families were fairly well off.

So here I go, selling again. I seated them in their own living room and put it to them bluntly.

"I have a great opportunity, but I can't do it without some help," I said. "I need to borrow five hundred dollars immediately if not sooner." At that time in my life, I probably could have borrowed a million just as easily. But the lieutenant was interested.

"How are you going to pay me back?" he asked.

"Simple," I said. "I'll give you ten dollars for every vacuum cleaner I sell in a one-year period, and I plan to sell a lot of them. You'll quadruple your money, but that's fine with me— just let me have the money, and I'll show you."

"Sounds like a good deal," he said with a smile, and his wife agreed.

It *was* a good deal—for him—it wasn't so good for me. But I'm grateful for the lesson I learned. I was so eager to borrow the money I was willing to offer more than was necessary to get it, and in the end it cost me. Suffice it to say I paid off the loan in a year's time, and they made a very handsome profit. But a deal's a deal, and I will be eternally grateful for their faith in us.

Adding even more pressure to the situation we found ourselves in, we had to buy a house in Altus, but we had no money for a down payment. When we found the house we were looking for—a new one—the contractor wanted to help, even though we couldn't make the down payment. Apparently we hit the right button because he remembered how hard it was for him to get started in business.

"Tell you what," he said sympathetically. "I'll sell it to you, and you can give me the down payment in six months."

We thanked him profusely, feeling good because someone had faith in us.

So there we went again—another "impossible" challenge. But in six months, I'd sold enough vacuum cleaners that we could pay the fifteen hundred dollars and establish ourselves as responsible young entrepreneurs in our chosen home city. We were feeling pretty good about ourselves, and on our way. For furnishings, we had made purchases at a used furniture store, and with a lot of imagination Miss Melba made it work beautifully. Nothing fancy, but to us it was Nob Hill, U.S.A.

While I worked at selling, she doubled as bookkeeper and repair technician, and I hired a sales crew to help me—only this time I treated them better. Before the end of the first year, we were a thriving business, making a comfortable living for the first time in our lives.

But I couldn't believe it when a call came in late one afternoon from the head office to let me know that R. J. "Jim" Sperry, Kirby's divisional supervisor, was going to be visiting Altus the next morning to inspect the facility and congratulate us in person. And he was to bring the national sales manager of the Scott and Fetzer Company with him! It was overwhelming to think about actually getting recognition like that from the people who ran the company.

So I cleaned up my sales office—it might have been a garage, but I made it gleam—and long after dark I realized the grass outside was deeper than it should be. After all, if I had a military haircut, my *lawn* should have one too. I'd heard stories of farmers harvesting by the light of the moon, but I was probably the only guy who'd ever mowed grass with a flashlight strapped to his head. I didn't make *Ripley's Believe It or Not*, but apparently it impressed the boss.

The dawn came, and I was up and at 'em. I had mandated that my entire sales staff wear their best clothes, and we greeted the dapper, impressive executives with some stirringly enthusiastic, slightly off-key Kirby sales songs.

"Son," said Mr. R. J. "Jim" Sperry as we walked inside, "this lawn looks like you mowed it last night."

"I did," I said, standing at attention and resisting the impulse to salute. This was top Kirby brass, remember, and I hadn't been out of the military that long.

Sometime later, I got a call from Casey Southern with the offer of still another life-changing career opportunity, and I knew it must have been on recommendation of Mr. Sperry. (When he'd paid us that visit, we had done everything but make the lid of the commode snap to attention.)

When Casey called, I had a feeling something good was about to happen. I've always been that way—psychic, psychotic, or gut feeling, I don't know, but it's worked out well for me.

"Tom," he said with more fatherly affection in his voice than I ever remembered, "I think we have a chance for you to become a factory distributor just like me. Are you interested?"

"Are you kidding? Where?" It didn't matter, really. I just needed to know which direction to travel, because I knew it was *up*.

"I don't want to tell you just yet. But I'll take you there myself. How about it?" He offered to go with me, help look over the new location, and see how we felt about it. All he would say was: "It's close to Houston, Texas."

"When do we leave?"

"How soon can you be ready?"

I was ready then and there.

Well, on the trip, as we got closer and closer to Houston, I thought maybe it *was* Houston. Wow! "Casey, you've got to be kidding—Houston is going to be all mine?"

"Not quite," he said. "But I think you'll have your hands full where I'm taking you."

Casey was right. Over an hour later we rolled into Beaumont, a sprawling city of perhaps 120,000. It was a territory ten times larger than any place I'd ever lived before, and I started making mental calculations about how many vacuum cleaners I could sell to such a vast population. Visions of instant riches were dancing in my head by the time we checked in at the Ramada Inn, and Casey suggested that we knock on a couple of doors that night and "see what the climate's like in this part of the world."

As fate would have it, the first house we went to was the home of a Mr. Mudd, who was very happy with his Electrolux vacuum cleaner and had no interest whatsoever in buying or even *looking* at a Kirby.

I hoped it wasn't an omen, but nothing could dampen our spirits over a celebration dinner that night. We also discussed the necessary start-up merchandise. Casey said it would take about two thousand dollars' worth for Beaumont, and he asked if I had that kind of money.

"No, I don't, Casey, but I don't want to lose this opportunity."

"Well, I can help you out, but here's what you'll have to do," he said, outlining a plan. I would sign my house in Altus over to him, and at the end of a year, I could pay off the loan and he would give the house back to me. There were no ill feelings about it at all, just good business. I'd tried to put him out of business once, and that hurt him. He wasn't going to take any chances, and I didn't blame him a bit. Melba didn't like it, but she didn't let it show. We said yes, and we never lived to regret it. Later, we rented that house out for another ten years and finally sold it at a profit.

A month later, when we moved officially to Beaumont, Melba found a repossessed, wood-frame house, not as nice as the one in Altus, but believe it or not, we bought that house for $25 down and payments of $123 a month! We may have had used furniture in the house, and used vacuums to sell, but along with it all went a whole lot of hopes and dreams.

"Wow!" I said to Melba. "Beaumont, Texas! This is where we'll plant our roots, raise our family, and conquer the world!"

The first thing I needed to do was set up a bank account with an aggressive banker. Jim Sperry, who had started out in Beaumont, had suggested the bank I should use, so here I went again, knocking on bank doors, hoping to sell one on the idea of buying vacuum cleaner "paperwork." I had a 120,000-population town and I was *going* for it.

I became Casey Southern's top salesman and then got promoted to sales manager.

It was one of my best sales pitches ever, and I'll never forget it. Here I was sitting down with the vice president of loans at one of the biggest banks in Beaumont, telling him what I needed.

"How much do you have in the bank?" he asked.

"A hundred dollars," I said, trying to make it sound like a hundred thousand.

"What?" he asked, looking up at me as though I were kidding.

That's when I turned on the heat—selling him on *me*, and not the idea of vacuum cleaners.

"If I bring you fifty new customers a month," I said, "that's six hundred a year. That's not bad, and you didn't even have to spend advertising money to get them. I'll sign these contracts over to you as loans, and you can turn them into car loans, home improvement loans, whatever you want. So I'm really doing you a favor by selling you this paperwork."

"We're not interested in vacuum cleaner loans," he told me.

"Well, let's do it this way. If the vacuum cleaner sells for two hundred, I'll let you keep twenty in a reserve account. This money will be mine, but I can't touch it until every vacuum cleaner is paid off."

Well, he began to soften up, and I think he even blinked a couple of times.

"It'll be my money and I'll earn interest on it, but it will be there for you to keep in case I goof up."

"Well, that sounds a little better, but I still don't know . . ."

"Wait until you hear the kicker, I'm not done yet," I said. "If I do all of that, I want twenty percent participation in the interest from you, and that goes into another account I won't touch until all vacuum cleaners are paid for."

"We won't do any such thing, Mr. Harken."

"Wait a minute and think about this. Don't you want to become president of this bank someday? How are you going to do that if you don't do something different? Give me a chance and I'll prove it to you. I'll do it, and I'll make it work." I was singing his song, but I was about to give him a heart attack.

Three or four hours later, completely flustered, the poor man nodded his head slowly, shook my hand, and said solemnly, "Don't let me down."

"I won't," I assured him, and I meant it.

I was in business. I'll never forget it, and neither will he. We both made a good deal that day. Things like that don't happen today, but back then I didn't know the difference, so I just did it. And I had learned it from my mentor, Casey Southern.

It took a long time to keep that promise, and for a while I thought I never would. No matter how many hours I worked every day, no matter how many doors I knocked on, no matter what I said to people when they came to the door, I just couldn't generate the sales to make this novel arrangement profitable for either of us. For the first six months, in fact, I had trouble selling a tenth of that number, and half of the few I sold were returned after one of Electrolux's hundred salesmen showed up to undercut my price and bump me out of my sale.

A few weeks went by, then one Friday after a long week with nothing to show for it, I decided to knock on one last door before trudging home empty-handed once again. A nondescript man answered the door and listened patiently to my sales pitch. But he didn't invite me in. Instead, when I had said all I had to say, he commented matter-of-factly, "You seem like a bright young man. Why are you trying to sell vacuum cleaners for a living? There's no prestige in a job like that, and no future, either."

Bam! His words hit me like a blow to the head. What was left of my fragile-at-best little dream world, as invisible to the naked eye as the dark secret of my illiteracy, came crashing down all around me. Too stunned to reply, I returned to the car and drove around in a daze for a couple of hours. Every bad thing that had ever happened came back to haunt me. I relived all the terrors. It was as though I'd been stripped naked, cut loose, and cast out into darkness.

What? No future? I thought. Had I been working for nothing? For *nothing?* Where was the purpose in life? I found myself in the downtown area of Beaumont, near the bus station, where I often picked up inventory and supplies. Still in a daze, I got out of my car and stumbled toward the rest room. A big Trailways bus was huffing and puffing and about to pull out, and it looked so inviting that for a moment I could visualize nothing but escape. I leaped aboard with no thought in mind but to let somebody else drive for a while. I'd had it.

Funny thing about that urge to escape. Most of the time it is brought about by God toughening us up by letting us fend for ourselves for a while. Nothing infuriates us humans more than being in limbo. Each of us is born for a purpose, and once we think we're on the road, we hate delays in getting there. But God doesn't work on our time frame.

There have been times on my road when I've been mad at God and times when He must have been mad at me. Early on, when He had plans for my life that I didn't understand, I rebelled, and we were at odds with each other. Too often when we get into that position we don't want the responsibilities that being without God forces upon us, so we try to run away. I believe it's good now and then to consider the responsibility God assumes for us all if we do right by Him. We should thank *Him* for not running away. He must get the urge every day.

During my escape attempt, I sat on that bus and, staring straight ahead, didn't see a thing. I didn't *think* a thing. I just rode fifty or so miles to Lake Charles, just over the Louisiana border, and got off the bus. After wandering the empty streets for an hour, then nursing coffee in a diner until closing time, the numbness in my brain began to wear off. *God help me,* I thought, *and I'll start trying to keep some of those old promises to myself. OK, God? And if it's all right with You, if it's the last thing I do, I'm gonna show that guy there* is *a future in vacuum cleaners. So lead the way, and point me in the right direction.*

My brain was clearing up, I was coming out of the fog, and

wonder of all wonders, self-confidence began returning. I didn't know where it had been, but I was glad it was coming back.

Then I got on another bus—this one headed in the right direction: toward home and Miss Melba and the boys. It was about three in the morning when I arrived home. Worried sick, Melba was waiting up for me as usual, and she burst into tears when I walked in the door.

"I thought you'd been in an accident or something," she said. "Where were you?"

"Don't worry," I said gently, giving her a hug and growing up a little more. "I wasn't shooting pool with the boys."

I was still feeling sorry for myself when R. J. Sperry invited me to join the other distributors at the next regional meeting. I didn't pay much attention to the proceedings until the very end when he asked if any of us had work-related problems we'd like to discuss. Like a fool, I raised my hand, then went on to tell them about my frustration in trying to establish a foothold in Beaumont.

That old salesman, impeccably dressed and confident as he'd been thirty years earlier, looked straight at me, his eyes reflecting the look of a winner.

Without any gentleness or compassion, he lit right into me: "Tom, I've known you for a while now, and you're a master salesman. You've proved it time and again as you've moved up the ranks, and you've earned the right to be a factory distributor. But now that you're among the elite, you're telling us that you forgot how you got here."

"What do you mean?" I protested. "I work hard."

"Well, you've forgotten how to fight fire with fire, how to beat them at their own game. Unless you wake up and start selling instead of crying about it, you'll never make it as a factory distributor. If this is all too much for you, we'll have to demote you back to an area distributor. I don't want to do it, but I will."

I felt like I had when that elementary school teacher had reprimanded me in the classroom, and I had put my head down, steaming with anger. But this time I wasn't going to take it out on myself by quitting. In no uncertain terms, Mr. Sperry had told me what I needed to hear, and I went back home more excited, more determined, with more life in me than I'd ever felt before. It was like getting permission to attack, and all I'd been doing was waiting for orders.

Once established in Beaumont, we even got invited back to Oklahoma to tell them how we did it.

I hired new salesmen with the same spark and drive I had. We even stole some of them from Electrolux by offering more money. We made better deals with customers to get their business for ourselves, and guess what? Within four years, we had the competition confounded and not a little annoyed, and I was sitting in the catbird's seat in Beaumont, Texas. I felt as though I had conquered the world after all.

There was only one shadow left in that dark corner of my

life, and I had been so busy running away from it, and so successful without ever having to come to terms with it, that I had tried to persuade myself it wasn't a problem anymore. But the simple truth was I still hadn't learned to read or write. I had taught myself to fake it very convincingly and write one-syllable words, and I could recognize enough basic terminology to feel my way through a contract, but I was becoming a highly visible citizen on various corporate boards in the community, and the time was coming when it would become increasingly difficult to continue keeping my secret from the world.

Melba had begun the process of teaching me to read in my late twenties, but I wasn't a very willing student, giving my denial of a problem, so progress was very slow.

On one occasion, after I had joked my way out of a blunder with my boys, Melba said gently, when we were alone, "Tom, our boys are growing up and learning to read. Don't you think it's about time their dad learned to read too?"

"I'm trying, Melba, you know that," I shot back, always on the defensive. "Just let me make the living and you take care of the small stuff."

"This isn't small stuff," she said. "And besides, you've been making some progress with one-syllable words—why not move on to two?"

She smiled patiently, as always, and picked up the vacuum cleaner credit applications I'd brought home.

"You sold *three* today, and you wrote in the names. That's good, Tom. See, I told you, you're getting better and better."

"Well, I don't know if I spelled them right, but I remember the addresses and everything," I said, still unwilling to admit that I had a major problem. But she'd heard all of that and went on.

"Let's see. You sold one to Jack's son," she said, then looked up quizzically. "Who's Jack?"

"Jackson," I said and laughed. By now, I could do that—laugh at my pitiable, illiterate condition. "It's the Jacksons who live on Highland Avenue." Then I gave her the address, and she filled it in.

"How about the Smiths?" she went on. "You wrote that one perfectly! Where do they live?"

"They're at 200 Jones Circle," I told her, chuckling. "If I could only sell to Smiths and Joneses, we'd have it made. I can spell those."

"We've got it made anyhow, honey," she smiled. "You're doing fine . . . but what's this Boo? Is that a name?"

"It's Boudreaux," I said, frustrated at remembering my futile effort to write it. "I'm never going to learn how to spell a name right!"

"The Boudreauxs had to learn it too," she said brightly. "Remember that."

And remember I did. In fact, right then and there, I set my mind to learn how to spell that name. I figured if I did that, nothing else would ever be a problem.

That particular family became dear friends, and not long ago I was visiting with the eighty-six-year-old father. During our conversation, I confided the fact that I thought I'd never learn to spell Boudreaux.

"Y'know, Tom," he said. "I thought *I'd* never learn it either."

But even then, Melba was the only one who knew my secret. She kept telling me that I had nothing to be ashamed of, but I didn't know it yet, and I was too proud to tell anyone I needed help.

All that changed one weekend, when I took Melba to help care for her ill parents back home in Oklahoma. My dear friend Dr. Robert Schuller asked permission to put this story in his book, *If It's Going to Be, It's Up to Me*, and it is there, but I want to relate it again here. If my words reach just one illiterate his doesn't reach, I want that person to be certain there's a little guy in Beaumont, Texas, who knows how he or she feels, and that help is within reach.

My in-laws were on the mend, but Melba decided to stay a while. Being youngsters, the boys were to remain with her, and I planned to get back to Beaumont and work. After making sure she had everything she needed, and giving her most of the money I had, which wasn't much, I prepared to leave for the return trip.

"What's wrong, Tom?" Melba asked, noticing that I seemed jittery.

"Well, you know," I said, giving her that only-you-know-I-can't-read look. "Would you draw me a map with some understandable directions so I can get home without any problems?"

"Of course," she said. "I should have thought of that." Then she drew some lines that seemed to make sense to me at the time, and kissing her and the boys good-bye, I was off.

Unable to read most street signs, I was always concerned about getting lost in big cities, and Dallas was the one big hurdle I had to get through going home. But Melba had given me the reassurance I always needed from her, so I felt fairly comfortable about the trip. Little did I know what awaited down that dark highway.

Barreling through the night, I was almost halfway along on the way to Beaumont when I saw that dreaded city limits sign, and Dallas swallowed me up. At that stage in life, my idea of hell would have been to die and go to Dallas. There were so many turns and intersections in this pre-freeway era, and soon, just like Job in the Bible, *what I most feared had come upon me*. I had stopped for gas and coffee, got "turned around," as the saying goes, and there I was, lost . . . hopelessly and utterly, in the middle of Texas, in the middle of the night.

Stubbornly determined but a bit frightened—of what I don't know—I plowed on, hoping against hope I would see something familiar, some landmark, some guidepost. There were signs everywhere, but in my panic I couldn't read them; the numbers and letters were meaningless to me.

That's the way it is with many people in life. When we get lost—physically or spiritually—even with signs all around us, we become confused, and everything seems to run together. We look for something, anything, to point us in the right direction. Years later, watching *On Golden Pond* as Henry Fonda wandered into once-familiar woods and became lost and panic-stricken, I understood the feeling. I knew what was going through the character's mind, knew the absolute desperation, and experienced it again.

I drove on, turning here and there, trying this highway and that, and after a couple of hours, desperation was creeping in along with the cold sweat. In those days, convenience stores and gas stations seldom remained open all night, only tiny coffee shops and diners. Finally the reflection of one loomed ahead. In the parking lot, a highway patrolman was pulling in to check a license plate with his flashlight. It was as if God Himself were standing there with a beacon.

In Texas today, it's called the Department of Public Safety, but then it was still the Highway Patrol. I almost ran this one down, so eager was I to ask for help, even though I was going to have to swallow my pride to do it. He turned toward my dusty old car as I came to a halt a few inches away and got out.

"Officer," I said hesitantly, taking a deep breath and putting on the best nonchalant attitude I could muster, "you're probably familiar with the phrase get-out-of-Dodge . . . well, I can't seem to get out of Dallas."

"What's the problem, son?" he asked, peering intently to see if I was either drunk or dangerous. I was neither, only illiterate, but I was sure he could see that too.

He was friendly enough and wanted to help. He began naming streets I should take, pointing to the main highway heading south.

"Excuse me," I interrupted as politely as I knew how. "I'm going to tell you something I've never told anyone."

"What's that?" he asked. "What's the problem?"

"I can't read," I said, ducking my head and kicking at a rock. For a moment, he just looked at me. I could have dug a hole and jumped in. Then it all came out.

"I'm lost, and I can't read the signs," I said, at the point of baring my soul, *wanting* to, in fact. "I'm a dropout . . . That's why I'm totally lost in Dallas."

He asked to see my driver's license, and I just looked at him and shrugged. "Well, to tell the truth I don't have one."

"You mean you're driving without a license?"

"Yes, sir. I could never pass the test because I can't read."

"Follow me," the officer said. I thought I was going directly to jail. But instead, he led me to an all-night truck-stop cafe on another highway, took me inside, and ordered coffee and doughnuts. As badly as I felt, I was ready for some of that.

The officer quietly explained that he had radioed ahead, and at designated points a highway patrolman would meet me and guide me straight into Beaumont. Then he added that he would lead me to the main highway to get me started. I could hardly stammer out my thanks, but I assured him Dallas, Texas, would always occupy a special place in my heart.

"That's OK. Glad to help," the officer said as he opened his squad car door to climb in for the first leg of my journey. Then as an afterthought, he paused and turned back to me.

"By the way, Mr. Harken, can I tell you something?" he asked gently.

"Sure," I said. "What is it?"

"I don't know how to tell you this, but you're not in Dallas . . . You're in Fort Worth."

I didn't know whether to laugh or cry, so I did both as he guided me into the night. I was deeply touched by the man's kindness and compassion, and somehow I would like to be able to find him and thank him again. But that night I was ashamed that I was a grown man and couldn't even find my way home. I realized how much this burden was getting in the way of my doing all the things I wanted to do. And I also realized I had nothing left to fear. I had let a stranger know what no other knew.

After that incident I really began to apply myself toward learning to read. By my mid-thirties I was getting a lot better, even carrying a book with me so I could read during any free moment. It was as though I couldn't read enough to make up for all the lost time. I was still slow, which was, and still is, frustrating, but the more I read, the better I got, and the better I got, the more I read. I loved the knowledge I was getting, absorbing it with gusto. I even got proficient at reading contracts, something even Melba finds intimidating. But they were of primary importance for someone who was planning on becoming a serious entrepreneur.

Melba and I have looked back and tried to analyze why I had so much trouble with reading, and without any expertise in this area, our best guess was that, in addition to amblyopia (or lazy eye), I am not a visual person. When I was a kid, I was so preoccupied with the world around me and so intent on staying in motion, that I missed some of the vital, basic skills that the average child gets. Then, once I got behind, I was lost. I had to develop other skills in order to cope with the routine of daily life. I became an expert at avoiding the many pitfalls that lay in wait.

I know it must be difficult to imagine not being able to read and, therefore, understand what life would be like walking in my shoes during those years. But Miss Melba, being by my side throughout it all, can attest to the fact that it was very painful. She has seen me at my worst, and now, I am proud to say as a fellow reader and writer, that she has seen me at my best.

9

A New Challenge

I hung up my vacuum cleaner bags and took up campers and RVs. People were coming to me to buy for a change.

❖❖❖❖❖❖❖❖❖❖❖❖❖❖❖❖❖❖❖❖❖❖❖❖❖

By the late 1960s, I'd been selling vacuum cleaners for more than fourteen years. We'd worked hard, God had been good to us, and we had been very successful—more so than I'd really ever dreamed. Sales contests we'd won had provided us with around-the-world trips we'd never dreamed of making, and I had even been inducted into the Kirby Hall of Fame. What a big deal that was for Melba and me. Tom Harken immortalized. Not in stone, but in carpeting, or the cleaning thereof. The word *overwhelmed* became a part of my vocabulary when that happened, and I couldn't even spell it. They gave me a plaque with my picture on it in bronze with my name below and everything. Other than the night I laid eyes on Melba, the hall of fame honor was probably the first time I said, "Wow!" and really meant it.

Now, we were carving a niche in the business world, and in

Texas of all places. I still loved Michigan, and Oklahoma, but the Lone Star State had become our home. Our sons were even growing up speaking Texan, which amused my northern relatives, but I didn't care. We were finally earning a comfortable living, and we were well respected in the community. That meant a lot to me. Melba had always known respect. I was still learning.

But as successful as we were, through force of habit, I was also still working the same long hours as when I started out. I just didn't know any other way, and I really didn't care to. Hours never meant anything to me. Never have and never will. Despite myself, I began to change. Me, the unchangeable guy. Maybe that's what security does to us—and insecurity—causes us to see life from different perspectives.

Whatever it was, I felt different. For a brief period, I'd been secure in the knowledge I could eat a steak whenever I felt like it, and I've always enjoyed my food. But God didn't put us here to consume T-bones all the time, and I just wasn't satisfied anymore. I needed a new challenge. I laughed the day *that* thought hit me. I thought I'd been challenged enough the day Melba insisted that I learn the difference between *fiscal* and *physical*. I had a habit of confusing the two, especially at tax time and when I went to the doctor.

The field of choice was somewhat narrowed with the ruling out of accounting and the medical profession. Besides, even if I was good at numbers I didn't have the patience to fiddle with them, and I almost faint at the sight of red Kool-Aid. I did know sales was my thing. I was born to sell. Commercial real estate was intriguing, and insurance looked pretty good—but there was always that big obstacle, my illiteracy. I had made headway in overcoming it, but not enough to make it in either profession. Both involved mountains of paperwork and months or even years of formal study. So I scratched that.

What *could* I do? The regional economy was booming, wages

were rising, and folks had more leisure time. All over the U.S., there was talk about a four-day workweek—what was this country coming to?—and in some of the factories up north, employees already were working ten hours a day to make their forty in a shorter period of time. Weekends were getting longer, and I figured a business that could take advantage of such trends stood a good chance of making some serious money.

It was about this time, while driving to a neighboring town one afternoon, I spotted a strange-looking vehicle coming toward me, and when it zoomed by I pulled over to the side of the highway and looked back at it. "Wow, what *was* that thing?" I said aloud to myself.

What had looked to me like a streamlined version of a Greyhound bus turned out to be a GMC "motor home," as they were called at first. I'd heard about recreational vehicles—they were the latest thing—but I'd never really seen one before; nothing similar to this one. Sight of that vehicle almost blew me away in more ways than one. I was about as close to being "in the zone" as a salesman can get. Too well did I know the feeling of watching others going places I couldn't go, having fun I couldn't share. I wasn't going to be left behind this time. I *knew* what I could do, and I knew it had to involve those deep-breathing motor homes. I had found my new line of work. Instantly.

The very next day, I began doing my own brand of research, talking to people, asking questions, learning everything I could about this new fad involving RVs. That was the zippy name people were beginning to use for them, and I liked it. In fact, I liked everything about them. When I heard about a big RV show in nearby Houston a few weeks later, I decided to attend and find out what all the shouting was about. I found out. Was I impressed? Did I see potential there? Enough to sit down on the spot and write a check for over $8,000—money I wasn't sure we had in the bank—for seven tent campers that I could sell for $1,995 apiece and up. I didn't need a math degree to figure out that I could make a lot more selling campers than vacuum cleaners. Even if Melba threatened to kill me when she found out, I was sure I'd soon be on the road to riches—in more ways than one.

"You did what?" she gasped when I returned home and told her the good news. She went right through the ceiling. (I think the hole is still there.)

"We're in a new business," I announced, trying to calm her down. "I bought six tent campers. They're already on the way here. I'm going to set them up over at Bobby Brown's service station and give him a $25 commission for every one he sells off the lot. We'll net between $300 and $600 apiece, maybe more."

"*If* they sell. But suppose they don't! Suppose you're wrong! Suppose we're stuck with them!" exclaimed Melba, tears of concern welling up in her eyes. Ever since the day we were married, she had been struggling to set aside enough so that we'd never again have to face another threat of eviction, foreclosure, repossession, or shut-off from an angry bill collector. "For years we've been scrimping and saving to reach the point where we can breathe a little from one month to the next," she cried, "and you're putting that much money on the line?"

It wasn't *that* much, but for once I didn't try to argue with her. I *knew* I was being irresponsible to go so far out on the limb without even consulting her beforehand. Still, I'd never had such a powerful intuition about anything. But suppose she was *right*. The stark reality of what I had done—on an impulse—suddenly hit me like a punch in the stomach, and I think I actually began hyperventilating. I think my high blood pressure began that very day.

But my instincts were right. Within a week, I sold all six of those tent campers, and we were in business—big business. I *did* clear what I thought I would. It didn't take friend Bobby Brown long to wake up and figure out he wasn't making enough money with that $25 commission, so I had to raise him to $75 for each one he showed, sold, and serviced. While Bobby was happy with what he was receiving, I was getting plenty too. In effect, he was a sales rep for me, plus, I was getting usage of the land and utilities paid. As far as I was concerned, I had pulled off a good deal.

I went back to my distributor with an even bigger order, sold it off even faster, then returned for more. The population of Beaumont was 120,000 at the time, and that first year in business I sold 126 of them from Bobby's lot alone. But this was a gold mine I hadn't even begun to excavate. I had been buying my inventory from a distributor who had a sales lot also. I was the only one in the state selling his products, and I was paying him 10 percent above the wholesale price direct from the factory. So if a trailer cost $2,000 wholesale, he was making $200 and not doing a thing. I was doing everything for him, and he wasn't doing anything for me. So I decided to pay him a visit and try to make a better deal. I might have fallen off the turnip truck, but I didn't land on my head. How stupid did he think I was? So I offered him a 50-50 partnership with no cost to me up front. I would hit the road, I told him, and both of us would get rich.

But he was very shortsighted. "I'm not going to do that," he told me. "This is my deal that I made with Travel Equipment Corporation out of Goshen, Indiana, manufacturer of the trailers, and that's the way it is."

He was belligerent about it, acted as if I was trying to pull a fast one, and finally I said, "OK, big guy. If you don't want to be reasonable about this, then I have to do something different."

I raced back home to talk with Melba. We got a map and began circling well-populated cities. Needless to say, if I sold one trailer per thousand population out of Beaumont, think what Dallas and Houston would bring. We got so excited we could hardly stand it. This was a no-brainer. We wanted to get that distributorship.

"We're going to go all over the state and set up dealers, and make that ten percent the other guy is making and not doing the job—all I have to do is convince that manufacturer to give me that distributorship so I can sell thousands of units." It never occurred to us that he wouldn't agree.

By now, Melba and I were excited and planning to "Go for it."

Next day, I contacted the president of the company, David Miller, and made an appointment to go and see him to show him some figures that would dazzle him. Another business venture, I told him. He said, "Come on," and I did.

In effect, this would eliminate the middleman and go straight to the source. Catching the next plane to Goshen, I paid a visit to the president of the Travel Equipment Corporation, manufacturer of the Lark and Travel Mate campers I'd been selling through my distributor. I knew I could do at least as well distributing campers myself—not only in Beaumont but in dozens of other cities throughout the state. Taking out a map of Texas with those unexploited cities marked in red, I told him with a straight face that they should be selling thousands of their campers in this territory alone, and that I was just the guy who could do it. I really believe I knocked him right off his chair because I had the enthusiasm to conquer the world, and these boys up north were not used to that. He said he'd think about it.

"Tom, I like what you've done in Beaumont, and you're right. We're not doing justice to the state of Texas. But I've got to have a day or two to think about it and will give you a call."

I wanted to close the deal right then.

I returned home and waited impatiently for his call. I was ready to get the ball rolling and keep it going. Always been that way. I'll never change in that respect. The call finally came, not soon enough for me, but he agreed to a deal—with one catch.

"I'll do it," he said. "But you're going to have to guarantee to buy a thousand trailers the first year."

"A thousand?" I gulped, trying not to sound apprehensive.

This time he knocked *me* off the chair. Those Yankees weren't as dumb as I thought.

"Well, if you can sell thousands like you say you can, then you should be willing to buy the first thousand. You got that kind of money?"

"Well," I told him with more confidence than I was feeling, "I've got enough selling power to do it."

"That's good—but you're still going to have to come up with something within the next thirty days."

"I'll call you back," I told him and hung up, already making mental calculations. A thousand trailers were going to cost me a *whole* lot of money. I needed about a million dollars worth of credit, immediately. I wouldn't need Melba to tell me that we didn't have that kind of money in the bank, and my credit wasn't even close to that kind of money.

So I went to my banker and told him the whole story. He said I wasn't strong enough to borrow that much.

"But you might consider taking in a partner. I have in mind a gentleman, he's been watching you."

He suggested I talk with Harvey Steinhagen, the local Texaco products distributor. He was from a prominent local family, probably one of the richest men in town—but the clincher, according to my banker, was that Harvey was as ambitious a plunger as I was. He was already a legend in Beaumont, and I felt a bit intimidated. But I knew I had a good thing going, so I relaxed as much as a salesman with fire in his belly *can* relax.

Harvey and I agreed to meet at the local Howard Johnson's, and in a typically Texas tradition we made a deal over chicken-fried steak. I told him what I had done, what I was doing, and what I was going to do. I had already talked myself into it, and it didn't take me long to talk *him* into it. Harvey was like a few other astute businesspeople I know. He could grasp the whole picture long before hearing a thousand words.

"So what's the deal, Tom?" he said, cutting to the chase.

"I'll keep sixty percent and give you forty percent."

Harvey smiled.

"No," he said in the agreeable tone of a friendly mentor. "You've got it backward. You may be doing all the work, but I'm putting up all the money, so it'll have to be sixty-forty on my end."

Harvey then shared another time-honored tradition with me.

"Tom, money talks and b_____ walks."

I wasn't offended. If our situations had been reversed, I'd be saying the same thing to him. I didn't like it, but I swallowed it because there was no question he had it and I didn't. But I was gonna go get it so I could say the same thing to somebody else some day.

"Sixty-forty isn't going to work, Harvey. How about fifty-fifty?"

"Deal. Let's go to the bank right now and get the money," he said, and we got up and did just that. Never did finish that meal.

We got our million-dollar credit line, bought the thousand units, and rolled up our sleeves to go to work. I became the president of our new company, Revedi, Inc.—named for Recreational Vehicle Distributors—with Harvey as vice president and Melba as secretary-treasurer.

But I knew we'd never be able to sell a thousand trailers a year if I kept trying to sell vacuum cleaners at the same time, so the first thing I did was make a trip to Dallas and break the news to my supervisor, R. J. Sperry; it was time for me to leave Kirby. I'd been with them for a lot of years, seven of them in Beaumont, but he was very gracious about it when I asked if he could find someone to buy me out. He did.

At that point, R. J. was in transition himself because he was about to become a major investor in a fried chicken chain in San Antonio called Church's Chicken. Another successful vacuum cleaner salesman named Dave Bamburger started that chain. Isn't that something! A few years earlier, Dave and I had sold vacuum cleaners together in Lawton, Oklahoma. R. J. asked if I'd rather invest with them, and I thought those two were crazy. Kentucky Fried Chicken had that market sewed up. Besides, you go to church to hear a sermon, not eat fried chicken. Some years later, when Church's was sold, I heard Dave's part came to hundreds of millions of dollars. Boy, had I been wrong. But I went on to do pretty well without it.

Melba and I made a little bit of money on that last deal, and before we knew it, we were out of the vacuum cleaner business.

10

Family Time

*On one of our vacations, I took Melba and the boys to visit
the church in Lakeview where my dad was Sunday school
superintendent for thirty years.*

❖❖❖❖❖❖❖❖❖❖❖❖❖❖❖❖❖❖❖❖❖❖❖❖

I was relieved to be getting out of the vacuum cleaner business, but at the same time a bit saddened. I knew I could sell vacuum cleaners and could always fall back on it if necessary. But now I could get used to people coming to *me* to buy something, rather than the other way around. This was really exciting. In the vacuum cleaner business, we had to keep coming up with ways to create that old want, need, and desire. In the RV business, they already *had* the desire to buy. BIG difference. And I loved the "new" way of selling. With my closing ability, this was a snap. A new day had begun.

We took care of that thousand-trailer deal immediately. I talked with Harvey and told him we needed to pull in some more investors. We did, and we formed Lark Trailer Sales of

Dallas, Fort Worth, Houston, and New Orleans, with a retail lot in Beaumont. Immediately, we set up these companies, with me as president, and began pouring campers into them. Also, Harvey was partner in a couple of Gibson Discount Stores, similar to Wal-Mart, in the city of Austin, Texas. This gave us more retail lots. In less than sixty days, we had seven retail lots in major cities that we were distributing to and making 10 percent, plus owning 50 percent on the retail lots. It was working.

Then, I started setting up dealers right and left in other cities. Plus, we were in every major RV show in Texas, and it didn't take long for the factory to figure out we could make it happen. They offered me four more states—there was Texas, then Louisiana, Oklahoma, Arkansas, and New Mexico. Talk about moving and shaking! We were getting a million-dollar line of credit from every city in the state without knowing for sure which direction we were going—but we did know we were going.

It's amazing the way other opportunities can arise.

We soon had six retail lots filled with those profitable trailers—five in Texas and one in Louisiana. Revedi also became a wholesale distributor, supplying five states. I mean, these campers were selling like popcorn. Sales kept mushrooming so fast that before long the factory in Indiana couldn't supply enough units to keep up with customer demand, and Travel Equipment Corporation had to build a new factory in Hesston, Kansas, just for us. Hesston Implement Company was located there and manufactured trailers and campers. It's a small community of Mennonites and Amish people, just like Goshen. So the workforce was already there. I tried to have it put in the middle of Texas, but they were already accustomed to the dedication and craftsmanship of those hardworking people, and I was voted down.

Before long, we'd grown so much that TEC began running short of trucks to deliver the merchandise. Wow! With the need for a fleet of interstate haulers, another door of opportunity opened in my mind. Soon, we were owners of a new trucking company. Melba had more work to do, and Revedi had a lock on the camper business in five southwestern states. RVs became so popular that car dealers began buying from me. Before I knew it, I was a dealer myself—a Mazda partnership—and owner of a Kawasaki motorcycle dealership.

In the early '70s campers were the craze, and Melba and I caught the wave at the right time.

Harvey was glad we went into business together, and I'll always be grateful to him for taking a chance on me. I didn't let him down. Eventually, a couple of years later, I bought his stock, giving him a very substantial profit, and we've remained friends over the years.

We billed our trailers as "the best vacation home in the world." As far as I was concerned, they were. To sell, you have to believe in your product, and I certainly believed in mine. On rare occasions, I'd take the family and head to the nearby lakes with one of the trailers. These excursions were infrequent because we didn't take vacations when I was a kid. We worked. That's all my father knew. Open the store, work, close, and go home—six, then seven days a week. He did take that one vacation, the year I sold all his coffee. Maybe *that's* why he never took another one. He was afraid to. Whatever, I never gave it a thought that we didn't go somewhere during the summer. That was for rich people.

But when Tommy and Mark were kids and Melba and I were working, I began to realize that even though we were providing for them, I was being negligent as a father. For the most part, they were happy little guys, but I could see it in their eyes—they wanted a dad. Something was missing when they'd blow out the candles on birthday cakes. I could understand this because later, when Melba would tell me about their little parties, I'd feel it too—an emptiness, the pull of deeply buried fatherly instincts. Gradually this love surfaced.

On one occasion years earlier, when the boys were reading pretty good and when about all I could do with a road map was unfold it, I had embarrassed myself by showing them a map and pointing to places I thought they might like to go. Tommy and Mark don't remember it now, but I made the mistake of putting a finger on a city in Texas.

"How about if we go there?" I had suggested helpfully.

"But Dad, we're already there," Tommy said. "You're pointing at Beaumont."

"You're kidding, right?" Mark chimed in.

"Yeah, I'm kidding, boys," I said, looking over at Melba. I laughed it off as she tried to smile that day. Tommy and Mark had seemed a bit puzzled, but enjoyed the joke.

It took a long time to get over that, but when the boys were twelve and thirteen, I began trying to spend more time with them and plan trips now and then. Sometimes we'd go out of state, but most times it would be to Lake Sam Rayburn, which was only about sixty miles from home.

But even during those trips to the lake, I was selling, visiting with potential customers, talking deals, so the boys were pretty much on their own. They had fun, but there wasn't much time spent in the father-son type relationship that is considered the norm.

Not to say that we didn't all have our good times. I was always tough as a boot on the boys, so they were not above laughing uproariously when old Dad committed some type of social blunder. During one unforgettable trip home from a Florida vacation, we made a pit stop at a highway gas station, and as usual, I hightailed it toward the men's room. The door was locked, and at that point I needed desperately to be inside.

The ladies' room was right there, unoccupied and unlocked. Voilà! I slipped inside just in the nick of time, yelled to the boys to watch the door, and failed to lock it behind me. I then sprang into the nearest of two stalls. Well, Melba and the boys were seeing to our dog, Tibby, and didn't notice when two ladies entered the rest room—with me in it and completely indisposed.

The ladies were laughing and talking, and inadvertently, I overheard more about their previous night's adventures than I wanted to know. One even requested that I share the tissue, which I silently passed under the partition. There was about a foot of open space below.

"You don't say much, do you, honey?" she said.

"Hmm-mmm," I squeaked in the highest-pitched falsetto I could muster. By this time, I had raised my obviously male-shod feet from the floor.

They finally left, and solitude once more prevailed. Within a few minutes, I was prepared to exit, and hearing a female approaching, I hurriedly locked the door. Well, she didn't leave and was soon joined by another woman. By their voices, I could tell it was the same two as before. They began rapping impatiently on the door, wanting in, trying the knob, rattling around outside.

"What's the problem in there?" one yelled.

By then, I knew there was nothing else to do but brave the

storm, so taking a deep breath, I unlocked the door, opened it, and strode out.

"No problem, ladies," I said. Staring straight ahead, I just kept walking—past those dropped jaws and surprised looks—toward the car, where Melba, Mark, and Tommy were all but rolling in laughter.

I was always good for a laugh, but my boys were always good for stitches and casts. They were very active, and while the usual childhood injuries didn't cause permanent damage, the maintenance at times was expensive for us. Melba complained that she spent more time in the orthopedist's office than at home. At one point, motorbike accidents alone must have paid for a new hospital wing or two somewhere. Mark once received a broken arm, and another time one of his legs required thirty-eight stitches as a result of such accidents.

But blame for one of the worst accidents falls right in my lap—or on my toes, as it were. I've always loved riding motorcycles or any kind of motorized two-wheeler, and one weekend after we set up camp on Lake Rayburn, the boys and I took to the hills of east Texas on some dirt bikes we'd brought along. Well, one of them dared his old man to race to the top of a sandy knoll. The resulting accident left my toes tangled in the sprocket and my blood on every pine tree within fifty feet.

Not critical, but very painful. The doctor finally got me all fixed up with medication and dressings, and we made it back to the cozy comfort of the RV, planning to enjoy a relatively quiet evening. Then, lightning flashes and crashing thunder broke news of a heavy thunderstorm blowing in from across the lake. Rain pelted down for what seemed like hours, and at one point, with the rest of the family asleep, I peered out to see that the lake level had risen and half of our stuff was floating away, including my boat. I couldn't let that happen, so in my underwear and with nothing but fresh, clean bandages on my feet, I waded into those swirling waters and must have hit every tree stump between me and that boat I was trying to save. As the pain shot through my legs, I kept thinking I shoulda let it float away. I'd told the boys, tie up the boat, tie up the boat, but they never listened.

Vacations were growing times for our family, and I tried to relax and enjoy them, but work was still where I was most comfortable and most successful. Revenues in the RV business just kept going up, and the company grew rapidly from only three actual employees—me directing sales and Melba managing the office, plus Bobby Brown in sales—into a large operation with several million dollars in sales at the retail level and several million at the wholesale level. I think it may have been sometime during this period that we became millionaires, but Melba didn't bother to tell me.

I can't blame her. She probably thought it would go to my head, and I'd dream up some other investment to make even more money, and she would've been right. But I was so busy working that I wouldn't have noticed the cash odometer clicking over anyway. Getting rich had never been my goal, and it never would be. I simply loved doing what it takes to *make* money. It was fun, kept me out of trouble for the most part, and provided a good living. Truthfully, it was my only real hobby.

A few years into this business of travel trailers, campers, and RVs, another big boom came in the form of customized van conversions from Ford, Chevrolet, and Dodge chassis. This started happening in about 1975, and what a shot in the arm. It was phenomenal. When Ford went on strike, Ford dealers were buying Dodge conversions. No one had ever heard of *that* before. In six months alone, I had sold over a thousand conversions to automobile dealers. Talk about prime time, or prime timing! Our company enjoyed being in the right place at the right time again.

But at last, in some ways, the RV business began to take its toll on both Melba and me. In order to make it work right, I had to travel constantly through our five-state territory. I had never spent less time at home, but with Melba so deeply involved in every aspect of the business, we were still close. We either talked late at night when I *was* there or conferred several times a day on the telephone, and this made for an even stronger bond. Our love was solid. I could relate to Melba. It was relating to my boys that gave me fits.

Any man who has been a typical son finds it difficult to be a typical father. In the first place, we're always under the impression that we've done worse things than they could possibly do, and in the second, we tend to expect our sons to be perfect— born with common sense, good judgment, everything. I don't know why we feel like this, but we do, and I think every father will agree.

God knows I wasn't perfect—far from it, in fact. But as with most dads, I expected my sons to learn from *my* mistakes. This must stem from having had a father who seemed not to make any mistakes at all. Just as I always tried to please him, Tommy and Mark always have tried to please me. I didn't succeed and neither did they. It's virtually impossible. But I tend to forget, and they tend to remember. At least that's the way I see it.

Still, I've tried to bear in mind that boys will be boys, and I'm very thankful we didn't have girls. Nothing against girls, understand, but if we had, I'd probably be a basket case by now.

As I mentioned, Tommy and Mark took after Melba's side of the family, and these guys were pro basketball material early on. By the time they were twelve and thirteen, I was looking up to *them*. I could have handled this better if I'd been able to read. But they were taller, and they could read too. All I could do was work and make money. Who knows, maybe those feelings had something to do with why I was on the road so much. Self-esteem didn't seem to be in my vocabulary during those years, and as long as the money came in, at least I had an alibi.

But I also had two sons and a semblance of fatherly instincts. I couldn't talk about it, though. It brought tears to my heart, and that was too close to the eyes, where feelings might show. I could sit at the table and spell simple words with Melba, but I couldn't express my feelings in the way I would've liked— hardly to her and certainly not to the boys.

So I resorted to the old toughness, the attitude I'd been all but forced to adopt in order to survive, the attitude I sometimes now used with employees, and until I'd learned better, even customers. My very basic defense mechanism kicked in, and unwittingly, I became—to them—a tough father.

Melba offset my toughness with her caring attitude, but I just insisted that she was coddling the boys too much. There was actually a time I considered sending them to military school. It's humorous now, looking back, but *then* the boys' devilment was infringing on business. To me, cost was always a factor—in everything, didn't matter what. I think I learned how to spell the word before I could spell my name. Tommy tells me he remembers one of my first cost-saving lectures following an incident way back at our first Kirby vacuum cleaner shop in Beaumont.

Daily routines never changed. When I was doing the door-to-door thing with vacuum cleaners, Melba would be in the back of the shop, performing all types of repair and refurbishing work on trade-ins. When not in school, the boys would be with her or playing outside, whiling away the hours until time to go home. This would get boring for them, and they were always coming up with new activities, sometimes to the consternation of their mother.

Someone smarter than me is noted for the saying "Time is money." Boy, that guy was right down my alley, and I've always adhered to that adage. When I learned that the boys' most recent prank involved ringing the service bell up front while Melba was working in the back, I almost went into orbit.

"Here I am out beating the bushes for a sale, and your mother is trying to squeeze another dollar's worth of profit from a worn-out machine, and you two are ringing the bell and running and hiding," I preached to them. "You're lucky I don't teach you a lesson by sending you to a military school."

"What's a military school, Dad?" Tommy asked interestedly.

"Do they get to wear uniforms?" Mark chimed in.

"You wouldn't last a day," I said, trying not to laugh at the realization that it might sound inviting to them after enduring my misdirected wrath for the first six or eight years of their lives.

Somehow, I always seemed to come around to understanding how they felt, and after a time my anger would fade because of the deep-seated guilt I felt.

Then they'd get into something else, and once more I'd fly off the handle. Melba *did* coddle them in my estimation, and by the time they were entering their teens, the idea of a military school was sounding better to me all the time. I was pushed to the edge one Sunday when I'd decided to do a rare thing and take the afternoon off. But it just was not meant to be.

At the time, we lived near a railroad track—I forget which side—and having gradually expanded into the recreational vehicle business, I had a warehouse and tiny office a mile or so down the track adjacent to the railroad switching yards. Unbeknownst to me, Tommy and Mark and their friends often hitched rides on the slow-moving freight cars, an extremely dangerous thing to do.

Tommy was about thirteen, and in addition to his and Mark's summer lawn-mowing jobs, he worked around the warehouse for me on Saturdays, sweeping and the like.

Sometime prior to this particular Sunday (as I would learn later), I had made a trip to the bank, leaving Tommy alone for a short time. Stepping outside for something, he had become locked out when the door shut unexpectedly. In looking for a way back inside, he discovered a tiny chip of glass missing from a window. It was just big enough to get a wire through and lift the window latch. He managed to do this, opened the window, climbed through, locked it again, and went on about his business without saying anything about what he'd done or how he'd done it.

Until my Sunday afternoon off. While Melba was doing something around the house and I was preparing to relax, the boys and their friend Barry, along with Barry's dog, Snoopy, were outside in the heat of an early autumn day, discussing what they might do to pass the time.

"I know," Tommy suggested. "The weather's so warm, I think we should go down to Dad's warehouse and have nice cold Coke."

"What with?" Barry wanted to know. "Cokes cost twenty-five cents, and I don't have that kind of money."

"Yeah, but Dad has an old Coke machine at the warehouse that takes only *ten cents*," Tommy said. "He keeps it filled with ice-cold Cokes, and we can always find a dime each just by scrounging around."

"But we can't get in," the younger Mark said, already thirsting for one of those frosty soft drinks. "It's locked."

"Yeah, but I know how to get in." Tommy smiled slyly, and that's all the trio—and Snoopy too—needed. They hopped aboard the next boxcar that happened to be moving in the right direction and soon arrived at my warehouse.

Now the first time Tommy had broken into the place, it was purely innocent, and he went unnoticed, but this time the whole group must have taken on a suspicious manner. I can just see them furtively looking about, then crawling through the window. What they didn't know was that an employee at a nearby auto dealership had observed the whole thing.

In no time at all, the boys and the dog were inside and sipping on their afternoon delight. Then Snoopy began sniffing around the big warehouse door and started barking incessantly. To discover what it was all about, the boys cautiously pushed the button that raised the roll-up door. There, crouched and waiting with handguns trained on them, were several police officers who had been in the process of surrounding the building. Those three boys froze, pale as ghosts and scared out of their wits.

Then they began some frantic explaining, saying it was their dad's building, and they were quenching their thirst. Finally one of them mentioned that their pictures were among some family photos on the wall of the office. This proved to be true, so the officers called me.

After the policeman identified himself, he said, "Mr. Harken, your sons seem to have broken into your warehouse to get soft drinks."

"On my one afternoon off in a year? It figures. I'm on my way, and I thank you for your trouble," I told him. "I'll take care of this situation and see that it doesn't happen again."

By the time I arrived, about all the young culprits could break into was tears, and they did that, especially after I told them they were going to jail. And they did . . . sort of. I loaded them up, dog and all, and drove right downtown, reading the riot act the entire way. As we approached the police station, I admonished them even more sternly, slowing the car and finally coming to a complete halt right out front. Those youngsters were quaking in their tennis shoes.

"See those bars over there?" I said, pointing to the cellblock portion of the building. "Those aren't *candy* bars, boys, they're made of steel, and behind them is where you're going to end up if you ever do anything like that again."

I let that sink in, then drove slowly away. I could've sworn I heard four sighs of relief—even the dog was glad to be going home.

Once there, I sent them around to all their lawn-mowing customers, telling them they would rake their yards for free.

To this day, I don't think those boys have committed any type of criminal mischief, and I know they've never had another ten-cent Coke.

As Tommy puts it now, my disciplinary methods were unusual but very effective. I suppose they were. Physical punishment was something I had experienced only minimally as a child. Later, as a parent, I had never even considered resorting to it. In fact, I can remember administering only one spanking, and even then it was by Mark's choice.

He was about ten, and during some sort of argument, he had spit in another kid's face. When the father came over and told me what had happened, I assured him our son would be dealt with accordingly. I gave Mark a choice: no bike riding for a week, no going outside to play for a week, or a spanking with a belt. He chose the spanking, obviously to get it over with and get on with a fun life only a ten year old can know. So I was forced to carry out my end of the bargain, as reluctant as I was to do it. And if I remember correctly, that reluctance helped make things a lot lighter on Mark.

The punishment I inflicted on them most was work, and both of them will certainly admit to that. But there was a time when I was accused of causing psychological damage because of my methods. A year before the spitting incident, Mark began experiencing recurrent abdominal pain. Melba of course took him to a physician, who examined him and performed various tests. The doctor's conclusion was that Mark's condition was all my fault.

"The problem is your husband," he told Melba. "His rigid attitude has affected his parenting methods, and he's causing the boy to be a nervous wreck."

The doctor suggested that I come in with her and watch a film that might rectify my problem. I didn't like leaving work, but I was concerned about Mark so I agreed to go. The film was about demanding fathers and left me feeling like a piece of junk. Guilt wasn't the word for it. There I was, blamed again, or so I felt, and I all but crawled out of that doctor's office.

Vowing to do whatever it might take to lighten whatever burdens the boys might have been feeling, I went out and bought a new powerboat, water skis, the works (I didn't know what else to do).

A young man named Tommy Carter worked for me at the time, and he knew about boats, so being busy as usual, I turned it over to him with instructions to teach Tommy and Mark about water sports. They loved it, and I also began striving to become a more understanding dad.

But the strange thing was, Mark's stomach problems persisted.

Eventually, he underwent abdominal surgery for a rare, ulcerlike condition that he had had since birth—and after that he never experienced any more problems. I later learned that the first physician we took him to had been considering going into psychology. He must have been practicing on me. Fortunately, he changed his mind and stayed with being an M.D. On the plus side, Mark was fine, some of my guilt was alleviated, and the boys enjoyed the boat for years.

My boys tell me their upbringing was probably about average, looking back on it now. They say I was difficult, and that's true enough.

"You were a good father, but during our formative years, we viewed you as being a bad boss," Tommy said recently. "We didn't realize you were trying to teach us to be good workers like yourself."

"Let's face it, Dad," Mark said. "You were born with stripes on your sleeve, even though you never gained promotion in the air force. But they made the mistake of placing you in the air police, and it must have given you an attitude."

"Sorta like giving Godzilla free reign," Tommy said with a chuckle.

"Yup. The air force lost a potential leader, and we gained a father," Mark said. "But sometimes I felt like the little army brat in the old joke who finally gets an appointment with his dad and asks, 'How do I transfer out of this outfit?'"

Like I said, they're really good guys; they've even got my sense of humor. And I'm proud of them.

If I've learned anything in all my trials with them, it's to continue to be a dad. All families have problems from time to time, but I think we get through ours because of our faith in God, and our faith in ourselves.

And we would need all that faith for the times ahead.

For working folks, Melba and I were going as fast and doing as much as any two people could, especially since one of us hadn't learned to read really well yet. Having been elected to several boards by now, including that of a bank—which I could hardly believe—I guess you could say I was reaching a certain level of prominence in the business community, and a level of awareness too. I began to realize I couldn't keep bluffing anymore, that I wouldn't be able to keep getting by with my catch-as-catch-can skills.

The up-front, in-your-face, give-me-the-money-and-I'll-double-it-for-you bull-shooting days were over, not only for me, but for just about anyone else who had skated on any kind of thin ice. I'd been there for many years, that's for sure, and while I considered my own situation, I also began to think about nameless others who must be in the same boat. The haw-haw-haw, good-old-boy image was *really* wearing thin, even in Texas, and I knew it was time to get real and get educated. Boy, did I dread that. I had to begin functioning at a much more sophisticated level in reading and writing, especially with the contractually accurate documents, and once more Melba came to bat for me.

I felt like a first grader again, but during the brief times I could be home she patiently tutored me at night for hours until I began to reach a point where I could do it on my own with no risk of major embarrassment.

At another level, for the first time in my adult working life, I was beginning to feel a little worn down. I didn't know I probably just needed a brief break. I was simply in a rut, but in my ignorance of such things, I even wondered if I might be having some kind of relapse, and the horrors of my childhood came back to haunt me for a time. Huge, beastly iron lungs returned to my restless dreams.

Then, at about the same time, the unbelievable of all unbelievable things happened—the famous oil embargo hit the United States and the world in October 1973. Nationwide fuel shortage, skyrocketing gasoline prices: The dream had busted. You may remember seeing photos of thousands of recreational vehicles sitting in a cornfield in Iowa. That was shocking. You could look out the window and everything looked normal, but it wasn't. You couldn't give a motor home away, let alone sell it. There wasn't anything we could do about it. Just before it happened, I began getting strange vibes. I decided to sell my trucking company, liquidate inventory and sales lots, and lay off employees immediately in order to salvage whatever I could before the bust hit. Luckily, I was smart enough to do it three months before it happened. I don't claim to be psychic, so don't ask me how I felt it. Everyone else thought I was running scared and had totally lost my marbles. As it happened, I was right on the money and had called the right shots.

At that time, I went to Canada to obtain a distributorship for selling hockey equipment, and to import CCM bicycles, the Schwinn of Canada. Man, oh, man. All at once I was selling hockey pucks in Texas, and setting up bike distributorships. Why? It only seemed natural to me. If you couldn't buy gas, you sure weren't going to sit home, so why not put the world on bicycles? Believe it or not, that lasted for about ten months and helped pay expenses. Then the RV business came back to life and is alive and well as of this writing in 1998. But after that experience, with things no longer the way they'd been, with the hatchet man having come and gone, I was ready to quit. I had gotten in on the ground floor of a brand-new field and gone as far as I could go in it, succeeding beyond expectations. There was nothing left to prove in RVs, at least not for me. I had come to a fork in the road, and as someone has said, I was about to *take* it.

But first, although we didn't know it, there was another crisis to go through, yet another hill to climb.

The camper manufacturer—which had grown into a major force in the industry as a result of the business I had brought to them—began complaining about my share of the profits. At the time, I was making more money than they were, due to the huge volume of sales. Soon, they were insisting on a cut of my commissions, and then they took over two of the states in my territory. When they began demanding my sales records and dealer contracts, I saw the handwriting on the wall, but before I had the chance to shore up my losses, they brought in a corporate hatchet man who decided to replace independent reps like me with their own company sales staff and "phase out" their relationship with me.

It was a nightmare period of strain, tormented by a sense of personal betrayal by the out-of-state business associates I had trusted—and enriched—but within a few months the manufacturer's ambitious new operation almost caused them to go out of business. It was poetic justice, but I took no satisfaction in their misfortune.

All this, coupled with my absences from home while our sons were in high school and the resulting strain on my relationship with them, had its effect on Melba too. Of course, she loved the boys as much as she loved me, and she did everything she could do to make sure all our needs were met. That alone was an all-consuming level of commitment she expected of herself, and at the same time she was working full-time in the business. It's no wonder she became somewhat depressed occasionally, and being the typical husband that I was, I resented it at first.

It wasn't any type of mental illness or anything along those lines, but we didn't realize that her increasing depressions were caused by a chemical imbalance that could be treated with medication. At the time, we had no idea what it was we were dealing with. Well, *she* was dealing with it mainly, going to work every day through it all, then coming home and crying. It was a very difficult time for everyone, and I wasn't quite sure how to handle it. But for the first time in my life, I had the opportunity to be there for her, and I was *there*. It felt good, and I'm glad it happened after I was finally mature enough to take care of her. I also began to realize that maybe I had taken Melba too much for granted. It did get my attention, and I've never forgotten what a priceless treasure I have in this good woman's love. It also served to refocus me and get me to thinking along the lines of staying home for a change.

I knew I needed to concentrate more on my family, perhaps try to recoup some losses in that area of my life, the area in which I seemed to have made the poorest showing. So with money in my pocket from selling off my interests in what had begun with seven tiny tent campers, I could afford it.

So in 1979, at the age of forty-two, I officially retired—for about fifteen minutes. I was bored silly the first day. I began to think more and more about getting into the "recycling" business—feeding hungry people on a regular basis. There were no gas shortages in the rice and bean business.

Within two weeks, of course, I was looking for that next hill to climb. And it turned out to be the tallest one of all.

11

My Third Successful Business Venture— Tacos

Casa Olé

❖❖❖❖❖❖❖❖❖❖❖❖❖❖❖❖❖❖❖❖❖❖❖❖❖

⚓I had hit it big in the commercial world of recreational vehicles because I'd been among the first businessmen to climb aboard this particular social movement and ride it to riches. Eating most of my meals on the road for a decade or longer, I had also been watching the emergence of a related trend: the booming restaurant business. Americans seemed to be evolving from a nation of single-income families, with wives who kept the home fires burning on the cookstove, into a society of hardworking, two-income families who preferred dining out to cooking at home.

I saw a golden opportunity to carve out an exploitable niche for myself as a restaurateur—although I wasn't yet even familiar with the word. Fast-food hamburger chains were already well established across the landscape, and entrées like steak and chicken were emerging as successful specialties in full-service restaurants for the family trade. But costs were notoriously high in the restaurant business, and so was the rate of business failure, so as always, I decided to minimize risk and maximize

139

profit by specializing in Mexican food, which was well known for being both nourishing and inexpensive. The profit in rice and beans is a lot higher than steaks and seafood. But skeptics had a field day when they heard about my plans to open still another Mexican restaurant in a town that already had many such establishments, even if they were small independents. With interest rates sky-high, businesswise it was the wrong time, they said, and the wrong idea.

As usual, I didn't let warnings stop me, and my transition to the restaurant business wasn't nearly as difficult as predicted. There was the usual grueling work, but I'd always been accustomed to the daily grind in one way or another, so I didn't mind that. After my father had left the grocery business, he had once operated a small cafeteria in Michigan, and I was aware of the satisfaction to be derived from providing good food to a hungry public. But never let it be said that I wasn't also aware of the potential for tremendous profit in this growing business, especially in Mexican food. A transplanted Texan by way of Michigan and Oklahoma, I had acquired a taste for Mexican cuisine early on, especially the old-fashioned Tex-Mex style that blends the best of south-of-the-border cookery with just the right spicy combination of Texas tang to make for mouthwatering dishes.

From the beginning, I had no intention of opening "just another" Mexican restaurant. Mine would be what I knew was a foolproof formula for success: good food and great service in a clean, friendly atmosphere, all for a price that working people could afford. I would go for 80 percent of the market rather than the 20 percent at the top of the earnings scale. It doesn't cost any more to give patrons the service they deserve. I'd been in too many restaurants where they didn't care whether you ate with them or not. The secret of my success in the restaurant business would be the same one I'd learned selling vacuum cleaners and RVs: I would treat the customers as if they were members of the family, give them a quality product, and make sure they left with more than they paid for.

While still in the RV business, I had toyed with the idea of one day opening a Mexican restaurant and had looked around in search of a modest but established franchise I could bring into Beaumont. Finally, I found it in Houston, Texas—ninety miles away. It was Casa Olé, a small but successful chain of eight stores. A couple of great guys owned the business. Larry Forehand was the founder, and he had been joined a short time later by Mike Domec. We all became good friends. At the time, I told them that I'd be interested in buying a franchise and opening up a new place in Beaumont. Whenever I was ready, they said, come on over and we would talk. So after my brief retirement, I headed off to find Larry and Mike.

I admired and respected Victor Gonzalez long before I made him my partner. We're also best friends.

Pretty soon, Larry, Mike, and their people completed the paperwork, we signed off on it, and I had myself a franchise. On the first four restaurants, I agreed to pay a 3 percent royalty. Forever after, it became 2 percent. With the details ironed out, all I had to do was pick a location and build the place I had in mind. I had already decided on a man named Victor Gonzalez to help me run it. Victor had emigrated from Mexico as an almost penniless youth and worked his way up the ranks all the way from dishwasher to the savvy manager of a Monterey House, a statewide chain. He had crossed the Rio Grande at the age of sixteen and arrived in Texas with a shoebox of belongings and made it pretty good. I respected that.

My family and I had frequented the restaurant Victor managed in Beaumont. Eventually he even hired my sons, Tommy and Mark, to work for him as busboys, and all the time I was watching him in action. The most efficient restaurant employee I had ever seen, he could park your car for you, then be at the entrance to open the door, bus the table, get you seated, serve the food, rock your baby, bring the check, and be standing at the cash register when you checked out, asking if everything was OK.

When I told Victor about my plan to start a Mexican restaurant of my own, he said that his job situation was changing, and while he would be loyal to his employer, if the opportunity came he'd be eager to work with me in any way.

"If that happens, Victor, I want you to be my partner," I told him.

In exchange for a five-thousand-dollar investment, I offered him a 25 percent share of the business. He expressed disbelief at my "generosity," but I told him he'd be earning every penny.

I took him to the bank to see if he could get the $5,000 loan. After telling Victor he couldn't lend him the money, the banker asked to speak with me privately. Victor waited outside, and the banker closed the door and said quietly, "Tom, you don't need a partner, you know that."

I said, "Yeah, I know that, but that's what I want to do."

"Besides, this guy's a Mexican," the banker said. That shocked me. Made me mad too.

"Y'know, it's kinda late," I said suddenly. "Why don't we talk about this in a couple of days?"

I never went back. I didn't like what he'd said to me. Still don't like it. What if he'd said, "Look, Tom, this is a white guy from Michigan!"

I liked Victor. I liked his work habits. I liked him just because he was a real person, an individual. That's the way I've always felt about people.

Victor eventually came up with the money, and we arrived at our own agreement. I told him about the banker's comments, which had infuriated me, and said, "As far as I'm concerned, you and me, we cut ourselves, we bleed the same blood. It's red."

"Me too," Victor Gonzalez said, looking me right in the eyes and smiling. "You've always been that way, Tom."

We've been brothers ever since.

The ideal location I'd chosen, and Victor agreed, was on Interstate 10, the link between California and Florida, not far from my first trailer sales lot, and just off a main cross street. I'd had the opportunity to buy the land two years earlier for $60,000 and didn't do it. Instead, a local dentist had picked it up. So I approached him about building a restaurant on it; I wanted him to construct the building. I told him I had money for the investment, but no experience in the food business, other than eating.

Then, we enrolled Melba's invaluable assistance, not only as our secretary-treasurer but also as our gifted interior designer and adviser on everything from uniforms to the proper tiles. You name it, she was back in it more than ever. We proceeded to break ground and build a spacious, colorful, sit-down restaurant. Victor and I personally hired and trained the entire staff in both preparation and service. While Melba always looked over the books and kept tabs on that end, he and I took turns manning the door as hosts for every guest until the restaurant was well established, and even afterward. We still do.

Our first Casa Olé opened on October 8, 1979, and was standing room only from opening day. But on that day I was the most nervous I'd ever been in my life. I didn't have to start a restaurant. We were already secure financially, so why take another gamble? What if the ceiling falls in and injures a hundred people? Holy guacamole! I even thought about what had been running through astronaut Wally Schirra's mind just before he blasted off in his first rocket: "Good grief, this thing was built by the lowest bidder."

But all went well, and that first week I greeted *every* customer. Went to every table. Asked them how their food was, if everything was OK. Finally, Victor told me we had a complaint.

"What the heck is the complaint, and who's the culprit?" I demanded, ready to put out the fire—and the one who caused it.

"The complaint is about you, Tom," Victor said, not knowing whether to smile or run. "I think you may be at the tables too much. A customer just motioned me over and told me our food is great and they love it, but there's some guy who keeps coming by every three minutes asking if everything is OK. The customers need to be left alone to enjoy their food. It's good, and everything is fine, so just let them eat."

What a day of reckoning *that* was. Here was this little guy telling me I was pushing too hard. So from that day forward, I tried to ask every *other* table how their food was. Do we learn through experience, longevity, or just common sense? I laugh at that today. But I'm still at the front door, and I'm still checking to see what they're eating and not eating. That won't change. You see, I don't just like this business, I *love* it, and I think it shows in everything I do.

That first restaurant was paid for in twelve months, so we built a second one the following year. At the time I built the first

Casa Olé, the Mexican food industry had been around for a long time but was still in its infancy. It was just on the verge of moving from traditional to flashy. In other words, more pizzazz, and I'm happy to say I added my own flamboyant touch. So on the third and succeeding restaurants, I got rid of the old, familiar red and black and substituted happy colors such as fuchsia, blue, yellow, and lots of bright neon—things like that. And of course, lots of young, enthusiastic, smiling people eager to wait on customers. Roughly translated from Spanish into English, *casa olé* means happy home, and that's just what we were making for the customers as well as the staff. The chain owners, Larry Forehand and Mike Domec, and their people went along with my ideas and have since revamped all the older units to the newer look.

By the time our third and fourth units were built, they were all earning unprecedented profits. I even started another Mexican restaurant chain of my own and called it Crazy Jose's. Casa Olé is the tropical bird that brought us, but Crazy Jose's wasn't a simple lark. It had a far greater purpose, and it worked for a number of years. I went into competition with myself in order to keep out national competition.

To me it was very simple. Someone was going to open another type of Mexican restaurant in Beaumont. We needed a new Mexican restaurant in our part of the world that had a more Santa Fe–style food, in other words, hotter and spicier, with plenty of pizzazz and flair, both in taste and design. I decided to put one in on Interstate 10. Spent about a million-six doing so. It was a beautiful restaurant. We also built two others, a total of three units in the same city with two Casa Olé restaurants. It kept out the competition for several years, and contributed to the closure of two existing concepts. We still have one Crazy Jose's here, and I look forward to adding more as we expand eastward in the direction of Florida.

For the first three years at Casa Olé, neither Victor nor I took a day off, with the exception of Christmas. We were there every hour of every day, before it was open, while it was open, and after it closed. We had the old basic work ethic, the work habits our generation grew up with, and we didn't mind, especially with people coming to buy something from me instead of me having to go pounding on doors for every sale. Boy! I sure liked it when they came to *me*! And come they did.

Never for a moment have I regretted the fact that Victor's original $5,000 investment has made him a millionaire several times over. He continues as president of the corporation, does a wonderful job, and is still my very best friend. In fact, marriages should be this good. Victor and I became friends first, then business partners, and it's a relationship that has lasted for over twenty years. In that time, we've had one argument, and neither of us remembers what it was about. All we can remember about it was that Miss Melba stepped in, and from that day forward we never had another argument. It wasn't worth it to face Miss Melba's wrath.

The fact is, we decided right then: "Let's just do what's good for business, not what either of us thinks is best for you or me." Miss Melba was a great help in many other ways too. If Victor and I took turns being the engine and rudder, Melba was the gyroscope. He and I are just two people, but sometimes we can seem to go in ten directions at once. Melba was there from the start to provide the stabilizing force we needed.

Victor and I still see each other every day, and we're in the stores together every day, making sure they're operating right. He still only takes one day off a week, and he tells me if I don't work, I don't get to eat free, so obviously I have to keep working too.

After almost twenty years since it opened, the first restaurant and all that followed are still profit makers. Our second restaurant—in Port Arthur, Texas, about twenty miles southeast of Beaumont—was another huge success. It had been open one year and one month to the day when I got a telephone call from my son, Tommy, who was working for me by this time. He informed me there'd been a fire, and the building was almost totally consumed.

Four walls were left standing. That was it. Tommy and I, along with Victor and a couple of other employees, started pulling timbers from the ruins while they were still smoking. By the next morning, the site was cleared and the contractor was preparing to rebuild immediately. I got the union workers and the nonunion workers together, and they did an unbelievable job of cooperating. The restaurant reopened twenty-nine days later, almost an impossibility. Even today, we're not sure what started the fire, but we believe it was the result of a botched burglary. Unable to get into the safe, the burglar or burglars torched it instead. It's my belief that when adversities like that hit, the best way to deal with them is just keep on moving. And that's what we did.

In following years we expanded at a comfortable rate, and the number of our Casa Olé restaurants has grown to ten, with no end in sight. The only limitation is self-imposed: I have to put each one together myself, and I have to run it myself. If I don't, they might not have the personal touch that makes them successful in the first place.

"America is like a gold mine," Victor is fond of saying. "All you need is a pick and a shovel, and start digging, and you will strike gold." You want to know why we're successful? It's because we are *workers*. Times may have changed for a lot of people, but not for us. We're still old-fashioned. We still believe in going to work early in the morning and getting home late at night, making sure our guests are taken care of and fussing over the food to see that it's just right. We aren't perfect, but we try to be better than anyone else in the business, and it shows. That's the reason we're still here. We don't claim to be any smarter—maybe we just work harder.

Casa Olé wouldn't be what it is today without Victor. His enthusiasm, his attitude, his loyalty, and his ability to work hard—he's an inspiration even to a workaholic like me. Victor has a great family, and I'm very proud of the fact that even though I'm not Hispanic and not Catholic, I was selected to be godfather to his son. What an honor that is for me.

"Coming in here every day isn't work," he says. "That word doesn't exist in my vocabulary. Some people go fishing, others play golf and tennis. I come to work. I enjoy it that much." True words of an entrepreneur.

But on one occasion, Victor complained that we needed to make some changes in order to shift some of the responsibility from him to his managers. He gathered the ten managers together and said, "Guys, I've got a gorilla on my back, and it's killing me. I can't even walk anymore. So I'm going to turn my gorilla into ten little monkeys so each of you can have one on your back. Now, *you* solve some of these problems."

They did just that. And they still do—not just the managers but every one of our family of employees, over six hundred-plus strong. We don't think of them as employees. We think of them as partners in a shared enterprise. Nothing pleases me more than to have a member of the "family" drop in and tell me about a new home, car, or boat, something like that. Whatever their dreams are. Something they're so proud to have purchased with the money they've earned working here. They come by every day to say, "Mr. Harken, I'm getting married," or "We're having a baby."

Several years ago, a young employee named Carolina was working in the drive-through, take-out section of one of our restaurants. She was very sharp, and even though she hardly went beyond high school, we saw that she had tremendous potential. So we brought her into the corporate office as one of our bookkeeping staff. She now heads our multimillion-dollar payroll department. One day, Carolina came by my office and said, "Mr. Harken, I want to thank you and Miss Melba for teaching me all I know about doing paperwork and handling money, and now, thanks to you, I have *this*."

She held up an American Express card. She said she was the first one in her family ever to have one. She was very proud of it, and we're very proud of her. I just love it. If that sounds corny, then I guess I'm a corny guy.

Not long ago, we had a retirement party for Juanita Martin, who had worked as a waitress for us for most of the seventeen years she'd been with the company. Juanita is a dear lady who is very close to us, and we were aware of the tough times she'd had. First, her husband died unexpectedly, then a son, and a daughter who left three young children. Juanita was faced with a lot of responsibility on waitress wages, but she made the best of it, and I'm glad to say we were there to help. When we started Casa Olé, we established a Defined Benefits Pension Plan designed to pay the same benefits to all employees, without their having to contribute one cent. The company would put it all in. When Juanita retired in 1996, we were able to present her with a check for $159,371.

As recently as April 1998, we distributed over six million dollars in pension benefits to employees. I've had people say, "Tom, that's not how things work in the restaurant business."

"It's the way they work at Casa Olé," I tell them. "It's the way things work in *our* family."

Juanita was not only one of the best waitresses I ever employed, she's also a pretty sharp cookie when it comes to investing. She took her check and immediately rolled it over into an IRA so she wouldn't lose a cent of interest. Smart lady. And by the way, she "retired" for about thirty days, then came back to work for us again.

The people of Casa Olé may be a family. But don't think for a minute that family members don't get upset with one another now and then. And don't think I can't be tough. With good reason, I'm known throughout the restaurant business as a stern taskmaster, and I run a very tight ship. At the same time, I don't expect any more from an employee than I expect from myself. No one who works for me works harder than I do. I'm not too proud to bus tables, wash dishes when necessary, even stoop to clean the rest rooms—and there's nobody better at it than I am. If my granddaughter was going to work in a restaurant, I would want to feel good about it. That's the type of restaurants we run. We hire a lot of daughters and sons of friends and neighbors, and I also want *them* to feel good about it. It's important to have standards, and ours are pretty rigid.

We have what is called a "lineup" twice a day, every day, for our store employees, the first being fifteen minutes before we open the doors for business in the morning. It's pretty militaristic. We line them all up, and we inspect them. We talk about what's going to happen that day and how we're going to make it happen. Do you look presentable? Do you feel well? Can you take care of our guests in the upbeat, enthusiastic way we know they like to be treated? If we run into one or two waiters or waitresses who've had a bad night, or who are having personal problems, we don't put them on the floor. And if they do have problems, we try to help them with those problems.

We do the same thing again for the oncoming shift at 4:45 that afternoon, just before the evening rush. Most of them are young adults, and we sometimes find it necessary to tell our people things like, "It's time for a hair trim." Or, "It's time for a shave." If you feel good about yourself, you feel good about taking care of customers. I've had mothers and dads tell me, "My son would never make his bed, and he never worried about how he looked until he went to work for Casa Olé." For many of those young men and women, I think it's just a case of first job and growing up. It took me so long to grow up, it makes me feel good to know that I've been able to play some small role in helping them along.

In return for their loyalty to us, I've developed a wide range of employee benefits that I'm proud to say have been hailed as models, not only in the restaurant industry but throughout the world of business. At an average cost of two hundred fifty dollars a month per employee, I offer health insurance coverage so comprehensive that my CPAs tell me, "You're crazy to do it, Tom, and you know you don't *have* to do it. Nobody provides that kind of coverage." But I tell them, "What's right is right, and that's all there is to it." If it's within my power, I'm going to spare the people who work for me from the same struggles that I've suffered through in getting there myself.

Me, Melba, and Trace salute during the singing of the National Anthem at a 1992 July Fourth parade in Beaumont for which I was the marshal. I didn't even have to tell Trace, three, to remove his cap and put it over his heart.

❖❖❖❖❖❖❖❖❖❖❖❖❖❖❖❖❖❖❖❖❖❖❖❖❖❖❖❖

But I'm still a demanding boss. If an employee straggles in at 8:05 on a Monday morning after two days off, I say, "Good afternoon!" As far as I'm concerned, they should have been here *yesterday*. And while Victor may have cut down to six or six and a half days a week, I still work all day every day of the week—and I don't stop even when I finally get home at night. If Miss Melba has the news on TV, I may keep one eye on it, but for the most part I'm reading over contracts and the like. Then, after getting to bed late, I wake up at about five in the morning and start all over again.

I'm not bragging, believe me. I know it's probably not good for my health—and other people's—for me to stay this busy. But I can't help myself. Ever since I was a kid, I've been on the go. I told God I wouldn't stop if He'd set me free from that iron lung, and I *haven't* stopped. It's just as well. With no Casa Olé to consume the boundless, unstoppable energy I seem to generate, I wouldn't know what to do with myself.

Another thing I'm proud of is carrying on a tradition started by one of my forefathers. When he left his native Germany many years ago and settled in small-town America, he was very proud of being an American, working hard and eventually starting his own grocery business. As a demonstration of his appreciation and pride, every morning, regardless of the weather, he would raise the American flag in front of our house and his store. That practice has been handed down from father to son for five generations, and I still raise the flag at home and at the stores today. The following poem, titled "I Am the American Flag" by Donald Robert Foisie, expresses my feelings about the flag.

I am the American Flag.
I am the visual symbol of freedom,
    courage, and hope.
I am the Red, White and Blue,

and am often called OLD GLORY, too.
I am the American Flag.
I am the symbol of you as you are of me.
   PROTECT ME

I am the banner of liberty, religious
      freedom and equal opportunity.
And our National Anthem is a song
      about me. It's the Star Spangled
      Banner by Francis Scott Key.
I am the American Flag.
   PROTECT ME

Yes, I am the American Flag.
      And I am the visual symbol of the
      heroes who gave of their lives.
And as they died, it was I that covered
      their caskets with honor, glory and
      pride.
I am the American Flag.
   PROTECT ME

I am the visual symbol of the
      Declaration of Independence, The
      Constitution of the United States
      of America.
And yes, the Bill of Rights.
I am that Star Spangled Banner in the
      land of the free and the home of the
      brave.
I am the American Flag.
      I am the symbol of you as
      you are of me.
   PROTECT ME

Every ninety days I replace the American Flags I have hanging in front of every restaurant. It costs a lot of money to do that, but we don't celebrate freedom just on the fourth day of July, we're Americans *every* day. We must maintain standards. Not only is it important, but it's the right thing to do. As we grow older in this business, it's most gratifying to have young adults come up and say, "Mr. Harken, I worked for you, and now I'm a CPA . . ." Or maybe they're doctors or housewives. But they all want to say thank you for not letting down our guard and always keeping our standards above and beyond many other companies.

I know that must sound self-serving, but if you want to help make the world a better place you can start out by teaching a young person to do the right thing. To quote something I read somewhere, I really believe a hundred years from now, it won't make any difference how much money you had, what kind of car you drove, what kind of home you lived in, just the legacy of achievement in the minds of the young people you helped. I don't think anyone can argue with that.

At the ripe young age of sixty-one—still feeling twenty and still getting thirteen months out of every year—I'm looking forward to the next millennium and future growth in our company. The restaurant business has changed dramatically and will continue to do so. The one thing that won't change and never will change is this: People want great food and great service at a reasonable price. To top that off, there is an abundance of young and enthusiastic people who want to be entrepreneurs. Why not open doors for them? It makes sense to me to continue to grow, from our solid foundation, at a steady, well-thought-out pace. I'm not interested in conquering the world. We just want a little slice of it, one restaurant at a time. Right now, we're in the process of allowing our management to become our partners and co-owners. The farther we get away from home base, the harder it is to be in every store every day, so we have to have top-notch, quality people who look at business the way we do, and proprietorship is the wave of the future. It lends one heck of an incentive. A good example of that is my good friend S. Truett Cathy, the owner and founder of Chick-fil-A. He's done it for years in the course of becoming a billion-dollar company. He was way ahead of his time, yet he's always been one of those men of God who never believed in opening his stores on Sundays, and I'm sure he never will.

Tom Harken & Associates corporate offices
This is where I, Melba, Victor, and the rest of our
staff/family work.

❖ ❖

Then along came a company by the name of Outback, which has set the pace for all of us to follow in the way of sharing in responsibility, and in the profits. I don't know the owners and founders of that company, but I applaud them. What I admire about these two companies is that they're not top-heavy. They don't pay themselves tremendous salaries, they share it with the employees. The world is changing at a very rapid rate. In order to compete and be successful today, we must keep pace and stay focused—on our customers, our partners, and our goals. To do this, we must keep greed away from the door. And we have to keep God in our lives. It's amazing, but it works.

I still drive a hard bargain in my business dealings outside the company, and I make no apologies for that. My word is my bond in the business world, but my word is *law* at Harken and Associates. And I'm not tolerant toward those who challenge me or question my integrity. I know it's a personal flaw, and I've worked to file down the rough edges, but that seems to be my basic character.

One day, I was coming out of one of our first stores. Here came a young lady on her way to work at our restaurant. On the way to the door, she was picking up paper that littered the ground here and there. I asked her name.

"Sara Peppas," she told me, flashing a beautiful smile. "You're Mr. Harken."

"How long have you worked for us?" I asked, and she said she'd just started a couple of weeks earlier. At the time, I couldn't have known that she was working three or four jobs and going to college at the same time. But I couldn't fail to see she was ambitious.

"Who told you to pick up the paper?" I asked, knowing I'd found a potential management person who was self-motivated. "Why are you doing it?"

Her reply was simple: "It didn't grow there, so I figured it should be picked up."

I liked what she said. I think she was about eighteen at the time. One day, a banker of mine came to me and said, "Mr. Harken, I want to tell you something that happened. While I was eating at your restaurant, I tried to hire one of your employees."

He'd been observing Sara and the way she worked. He asked her if she would consider going to work at the bank for more money than she was making. Her reply shocked him, and that's why he was telling the story.

"I work for Mr. Harken," she told the banker. "He's in the restaurant now, so why don't I just go ask him if it'll be all right?"

Well, he knew right away that he'd stuck his foot in his mouth, and he was afraid she was going to tell me, so he figured he'd better volunteer the information first.

But Sara stayed with us, thankfully, and as time went by, she worked her way up in the company. I must admit she was a very independent young lady, and at that point, I hadn't quite learned how to handle people like her. Melba was independent, but in a different sort of way. Sara had an attitude about her independence. I loved it and hated it at the same time. We had tried to fix her up with one of our sons, but she wasn't interested. It's just as well. She probably would have killed either of them by now.

She was managing a restaurant with sales of two million per year and doing a fantastic job of putting those two-digit numbers on the bottom line when she announced her marriage to a great guy named Jeff Lake, who happened to be our maintenance man. She wanted to get married in our backyard. No problem at all. I was best man, and Miss Melba was maid of honor.

Eventually, Sara announced she was expecting a child. I accepted the news both with happiness and dread because I knew that meant she would have to slow down and would not be in the stores all the time. Of course, that was no business of mine, but she had become like a daughter to us, and I probably voiced my opinion regarding something or other too many times. Anyway, for some reason, and I'm sure with absolute justification, she stopped talking to me. She did her work, and was perfectly civil to the customers and employees, but she wouldn't speak to me. This went on and on for days, and finally I'd had enough.

"Sara," I told her one morning. "I'm still the boss, and if you can't communicate with me, something is going to happen. I've had enough of this."

The next time I walked into her restaurant, I got the cold shoulder again.

"OK, that's it. I've never fired anyone in my life. Sara, you are going to be the first," I said quietly, forgetting about those vacuum cleaner salesmen in my past. "You're fired."

Her reply came back like a bolt of lightning.

"You can fire me," she said. "But I'm not leaving!"

Well, that made me even madder, and not knowing what else to do at the time, I stormed out, leaving rubber on the concrete.

About three hours later, I got a call from my son, Tommy, who worked at the same location.

"Whatever you do, Dad, I don't think you should come back to this store today," he said.

"You mean Sara's still there?" I asked incredulously.

"Yep, and that's not all . . ."

"That's it," I said, cutting him off. "I'll be right there."

When I walked in, to my amazement, it looked like a big flower shop. There were dozens and dozens of flower arrangements and potted plants, all of them bearing signs saying things like, "Tom is wrong" and "Sara is right." And of course Sara was standing there with a big smile on her face. I looked at her and said, "Can we talk?"

"Of course," she said. "If you're willing to listen."

Man, oh, man! That woman made me furious. I agreed, and we talked, and to this day I'm not even sure what the argument was about, but I know I didn't win it, except for the fact that I still have one of the best employees anyone could have. She ended up being a vice president of the company, and now is my special assistant. She has a handsome eleven-year-old son, and a husband who has to be one of the most easy going guys I ever met, because not only is she smart, she is an individualist in every possible way, and we all love her for it. I might add, I've never ever fired anybody since.

Our public relations practices have always been generous. For one thing, I believe in earning a good living and giving a portion of it back, and for another, it's just good business. I've always cultivated cordial relationships with community groups and individuals. In each community where we open new restaurants, we ask people, "What local charitable organization needs help?" That's who we select and work with to help them achieve their goals with cash donations or a continuing program of support to help that organization. Generous? Yes. Good business? Of course.

In one community, I went to a local city hall for some permit or other. The police department was nearby, and I noticed its run-down condition. Once I called attention to that fact, it jarred them out of their lethargy, and I got the ball rolling toward a new police station by contributing the first five thousand dollars. They got moving right away.

In the same way, we work with local schools to make sure good kids get the recognition they deserve—and a free meal from one of our restaurants. Students in all surrounding area school districts can receive such certificates as our "Cool School Kid Award," good for a free child's meal—and they get to keep the award and frame it. A similar program at our Crazy Jose's franchise utilizes what we call a "Golden Pepper Award," and it serves the same purpose. Of course, the little kids can't drive themselves to the restaurants, but they're so proud of their awards they want their whole families to come in and eat with them. So we'll end up giving one child's plate away and selling four or five meals.

We also recognize graduates of the local Drug Abuse Resistance Education (DARE) programs that are taught in the grade schools. Each of these kids gets a free order of nachos and a soft drink if they take their certificates to the local Casa Olé. If they or their family and friends happen to order additional menu items, and pay for it, we don't protest.

Special placards on the tables of our restaurants honor moms on Mother's Day, dads on Father's Day, and the flag on the Fourth of July. And with a customer response card handed out by the staff to every customer, we follow up on comments and suggestions—if I haven't already taken care of it through my personal conversations with customers at their tables. I always make it a point to go around and speak to everyone, kissing babies and shaking hands. We get back thousands of comment cards a week. I employ a full-time person just to read and act on customer comments.

Our company is stronger today than ever before, and we don't intend to lower our standards. I was told one time by one of my great mentors: If your shadow stops, you stop, so keep moving. Believe me, we're going to keep moving. What an unbelievable journey this has been, and it gets better every day. It's not without some challenges, and the hills are a little harder to climb sometimes, but after you reach the top of one hill and look into the next valley, it's always worth it. So climb your hill. Look into your valley. I challenge everyone reading this today to make this a better place for all.

In keeping with this, over the years since our first restaurant opened, I've become a fixture as prominent as a piñata at a party at Casa Olé. Together with seeing that things run smoothly, I've been the official greeter at the door and the glad-handing emcee of the show. I've staged new-car giveaways in celebration of our restaurant anniversaries, free dinners for a year to grandmas and grandpas who win certain contests, and any number of other promotional events. A favorite pastime is hosting special events for children. We even have a mini-Casa Olé restaurant—big, heavy-duty playhouse size—mounted on a trailer, and we use it as a float in parades.

Early on in our adventure with the restaurant business, we were accumulating some sizable deposits and assets, and I felt I could get a better banking deal if we put our account up for bid. So I went to three banks, and all of them seemed eager to consider my proposal. I told each that they had some competition and that I would like to have their answer to my proposal Monday morning. I told one to come in at nine, one at ten, and one at eleven. What I didn't let them know is that I was aware of the fact the following Monday was a bank holiday. I just wanted to see if there was anyone who worked like we work.

Bank #1 called and apologized, said Monday was a holiday and could they see us Tuesday. I didn't take the call. The receptionist did, and I wasn't interested in talking further with that one. Bank #2 made a similar move, or non-move you might say.

I didn't hear from Bank #3, and lo and behold they showed up right on the button at eleven o'clock Monday morning. They were wearing their golf duds and ready to head out for a game, but they decided to check in with me first. They were afraid not to show up, and said as much. I'm still with that bank today. After branching out all over Texas this past year, this bank became affiliated nationally. At one point I was asked to appear at one of their conventions and give a talk on how they got my business. I was more than happy to accommodate them because it demonstrates perfectly how going the extra mile—or the extra day—can help you get business, and *keep* it. The three young loan officers who came by on that long-ago day are now presidents of different banks. We often talk and laugh about it. At that point in my life, bankers were plentiful, and I wasn't about to be intimidated by one. And if the truth were known, I probably gave them a pretty hard time. And in some cases, maybe they deserved it. But let me add that a good banking association is invaluable to any business.

As with bankers, your lawyers need to be something special, too, and believe me, mine are, especially Benny Hughes. I now have various lawyers for a variety of specializations, but my friend and confidant Benny became my attorney twenty-seven years ago when a person usually needed only one. Benny is a lawyer's lawyer and has always led me in the right direction. I'll never forget the lesson he taught me concerning a certain company that is known for being very difficult to deal with—the toughest in the industry. Early on, in my zeal to make a particular deal, I may have signed a lease agreement with this company. I'll probably still owe them money after I cash in my chips in this world.

"If you ever sign another of their lease agreements without letting me read it, I'm quitting," my attorney said.

Well, I certainly didn't want Benny to quit, so I started letting him read everything but my telephone messages. After that, I took him so seriously that when he finally retired, I begged and pleaded with him to come out of retirement and continue to be my counsel. He did . . . and Benny's wife has thanked me for it many times.

I've always surrounded myself with outstanding people, who are not only smart but good friends too. Along with a good attorney, you have to have good CPAs. We've only had a couple on this journey, and I must say without their constant advice and sometimes very heated arguments, we never would have made it. Still, the amazing thing to me is who or what is an actuary? Even the government isn't sure what they do. But I have one, or better yet he has me.

Over the years, American commerce has progressed in some cases from one-man shows to three-ring circuses. I'm reminded of that old cliché about having to call a board meeting before carving a Thanksgiving turkey. But today, hardworking, qualified associates not only are a necessity, they are a blessing. No matter how energetic, effective or efficient the owner, there must be qualified employees who are capable of thinking for themselves. That is one of the traits we seek in those we hire.

Some people say our managers become "Harkenized," but who's to say whether that's good or bad, especially when the full story may not be known? Most of those who have left our employment have gone on to better themselves because of the valuable training they received with us. I've regretted losing a lot of these individualists, but I'm always pleased when they call me and say, "What you taught me five and ten years ago, I'm still applying today, and it works."

I love to hear that, and it gives me pleasure in knowing I had a small part in their business development. When they're having to worry about the bottom line, the shoe is on the other foot.

I'm still trying to learn to hit a happy medium so that I don't lose any more of these high-caliber individuals. It's great to see them climb that ladder of success, but darn it, I've trained hundreds, and I think it's time I kept all of them. Maybe I wouldn't have lost any of those guys if I'd been less militaristic, or just not so darned *motivating*. I have only myself to blame. I made them want more out of life, and they *went* for it. If someone can benefit by moving on, then I'll be the first to shake his hand, albeit reluctantly.

One of our "keepers" is a young man who came from Mexico and went to work for us. He rode a bicycle to and from the job every day, and he washed dishes. After a time, he expressed a desire to learn to cook, and he has turned out to be one of the finest, most talented people I know. He's our main chef, and takes a lot of pride in what he does. So do we, and so do his parents. He loves what he's doing, and that is creating new recipes for our tens of thousands of customers to enjoy.

One of my greatest pleasures is doing television commercials with my grandchildren and other specially selected kids from the community. They have dubbed me "Poppee" in these commercials, and the added bonus is that thousands of kids now recognize me as that grandfatherly type of guy. In the restaurants, on the street, and in the supermarket, kids call me

Poppee, sensing the kind of loving warmth I didn't have to give when my own sons were growing up. But in my later years, I sure turned out to be a hit with every other child in town, greeted with hugs wherever I go. A busload of them can keep me occupied 'til the school bell rings.

Proud Poppee
Victor and my grandson, Trace, help "Poppee" out
with a Casa Olé commercial.

❖❖❖❖❖❖❖❖❖❖❖❖❖❖❖❖❖❖❖❖❖❖❖❖

Then, unintentionally to be sure, I found myself becoming something of a celebrity around town among the grown-ups too. Suddenly, I was everywhere, from banks to boardrooms to the lead car in patriotic parades and cutting the ribbons at store openings to giving keynote addresses at local dinners. I was meeting myself coming and going, and often beside myself with excitement. The success of the restaurants led to many opportunities, especially for the highly visible—and hammy—company spokesman, and I didn't mind a bit. I still knew how to create those old wants, needs, and desires, and I employed every method I'd ever learned from the masters and the mentors. The more publicity, the more business, and the more business, the more people we could help. That's really the way I looked at it, and still do.

By 1990, with a widening circle of friends in higher and higher places, from business to government and back again, I was fairly well known in the state, and if it hadn't happened so slowly and naturally in the course of my work, I would have felt completely out of my depth. Even so, I was still amazed. But I had never felt so much confidence in myself, never been so sure of who I was and what I had to offer.

I had become a success in three different fields, and a millionaire, when I could barely read and write. Except for my beloved wife—and a compassionate policeman on the streets of Fort Worth, Texas—there was no one who knew the secret of my illiteracy, let alone the story of my long battle to conquer it. It was the one remaining shadow in my life, and I knew I would have to shine the light on it at last.

12

"It Is Time to Tell the Story"

Me, Melba, and Sara Lake (second from right) bring a Horatio Alger Scholar to Dr. Schuller's Hour of Power *program.*

❖❖❖❖❖❖❖❖❖❖❖❖❖❖❖❖❖❖❖❖❖❖❖❖❖❖

☙·I *could* say it all began on November 15, 1991, but the truth is it started a lot earlier and was much more than a beginning. Everything Melba and I had ever worked for, and suffered for, culminated that day, when I received notification that I was to be a recipient of the prestigious Horatio Alger Award. It was in the form of a personal letter from none other than Dr. Norman Vincent Peale.

A longtime hero and mentor of mine, although I never had the pleasure of meeting him, Dr. Peale was not only a revered clergyman, author, and confidant of world leaders, he was cofounder of the Horatio Alger Association. In the old days while driving on daily calls, I had listened to Dr. Peale's inspirational and upbeat messages on radio and had seen him on store-window TV. His classic work *The Power of Positive Thinking*, one of the most successful volumes ever published, was the first book I actually read cover to cover. Becoming literate so late in life, I was probably the last of my generation to do so, but its message of self-help through prayer and positive thinking had a profound effect on me, just as Dr. Robert Schuller's books would later in my life.

From scraps of information picked up here and there, I had been aware of some of Dr. Peale's life story. He had been born just before the turn of the century in rural Bowersville, Ohio. His father was a medical doctor called to preach, and the family moved around a lot. As a youngster, Norman helped earn money by delivering newspapers, working in a grocery store, and selling pots and pans door-to-door. I could identify with all of that. In fact, I have to laugh now when I think of it, but at the time, I had the gall to compare myself to that great man. Yet it wasn't in an audacious way; I think it was more like *wishing* to be like him. I always wanted to believe we had something in common, Dr. Peale and I. He had that way about him, a certain empathy, and of course others felt it, too, millions of others. In my case, I suppose it was his background in newspaper routes, the grocery business, and door-to-door selling. Not much to go on, true, but at least it was something. The example of his life inspired me to believe that even someone who had done no more than I was doing could better himself and make something of his life.

Was I impressed when Dr. Peale's letter arrived? You bet I was! For a good fifteen minutes I just sat there and stared at it, more overwhelmed with the signature of the messenger than with the message. Then what Dr. Peale was saying actually began to sink in.

I was somewhat aware of the Horatio Alger Association. I knew it provides scholarships to deserving young people. And I knew it honors people who have pulled themselves up by their own bootstraps to succeed in America's glorious and incomparable free enterprise system. And I knew that these honorees are men and women who typify principles embodied by heroes of famous stories created in the 1800s by motivational writer Horatio Alger.

I'd always thought those selected as recipients of the Horatio Alger Award had to be famous. Famous? Boy, was Tom Harken far from being famous! But there was the letter with that red, white, and blue Horatio logo and signed by Dr. Peale himself. I almost couldn't believe it. I think readers will understand my disbelief, not as skepticism or mistrust, but rather a yearning to believe something so totally and completely, simply in order to abandon oneself to the pure joy of experiencing it fully. Sitting there in the privacy of my office that day, I actually licked my finger and smeared the signature to see if it was real. It was, and I rushed out to the reception area holding the letter in one hand and pointing to it with the other.

"Can you believe this?" I exclaimed excitedly to all, my voice carrying up and down the hallways and into the offices. "A letter from Dr. Norman Vincent Peale! I got a letter from Dr. Norman Vincent Peale!"

"Who's that?" one very young employee asked.

"Is he that famous heart surgeon?" another wanted to know.

Was anyone *that* young? I think that's when I began to feel my age.

No matter. I explained patiently to my youthful staff, and they were suitably impressed. But later at home when I told Melba, she was excited but somehow not too surprised. Not much escapes these eagle eyes of mine, but it wasn't until this moment that I realized she'd had something to do with my receiving the award. Quite a bit, as it turned out. With some of our close friends and several of our staff, Melba had been working behind the scenes to make it all happen. From hunger to Horatio—it was to become the theme of a story that demonstrates how God indeed works in mysterious ways His wonders to perform.

Along with Dr. Norman Vincent Peale, there was another "doctor" involved—Dr Pepper. All I knew about this world-famous soft drink was that its famous trademark didn't have a period after the Dr, and it tasted good with just about everything. Three years earlier, unknown to me, the famous chairman emeritus of Dr Pepper, W. W. Clements and trucking magnate John Rollins had been looking around for someone who might meet the Horatio Alger Award requirements. In addition to being involved with the Dr Pepper Museum and his Free Enterprise Institute in Waco, Texas, W. W. also is chairman emeritus of the Horatio Alger Association and heads its membership nomination committee.

A resident of Dallas, known from childhood as "Foots" to his friends because his feet grew up before he did, W. W. started out as a route man for Dr Pepper and rose through the ranks to the top. Eventually, largely due to his vision, leadership, and decision-making abilities, he took his favorite beverage from Waco, Texas, to the world. Foots had won the Horatio Alger Award himself in 1980.

It so happened that Foots's stepson, David Thomas, is a good friend and one of my brokers. David, who over the years had become aware of some of my story, later said he immediately thought of me when Foots asked him if he knew anyone in this part of the world with a Horatio Alger–type background. It's true that I have overcome some adversities in a Horatio Alger–like way—and David didn't even know I'd been illiterate—but I attribute whatever I've accomplished to *enablement* (most certainly not ennoblement) by a higher power. I always feel a bit uncomfortable when I'm being praised, and I still give all the credit to God and to my wife. So it's just as well that the association's selection and investigative process for potential members is confidential and unknown to the one being considered. Otherwise, I would have insisted they give it to Melba.

As it was, she could hardly wait to break the news to me. She'd been sitting on this secret for three years! That's how long I'd been up for consideration, and each of the two years previous had seen other, no doubt worthier candidates, chosen. No problem. As I would declare during the awards proceedings, "I don't feel I deserve the Horatio Alger Award, but now that I have it, I'm not giving it back."

Together, David Thomas and his colleague at the time, Thomas Polk, another close friend and financial consultant, had composed a letter of nomination, recommending me for the award.

Now I understood why David had invited us to a special dinner party with his stepfather when Foots and his lovely wife, Virginia—David's mom—visited Beaumont. He was checking me out.

Melba showed me a copy of David and Tom's letter of nomination, and a double-handful of correspondence written by distinguished friends on my behalf. It was embarrassing to read about myself in such glowing terms. These two- and three-page letters were written to Foots and the Alger Association from practically every VIP I'd ever met. There was one from U.S. Senator Phil Gramm, for gosh sake, and another from Texas governor Bill Clements! Among others were letters from such friends and mentors as Ben Rogers of the famous Rogers Brothers family; Beaumont mayor Maury Meyers; Lamar University chancellor George McLaughlin; Lynn Draper, at the time chairman of Gulf States Utilities. I could hardly finish reading them—but at last it wasn't because I couldn't read. It was from being so overwhelmed with gratitude and humility. As the old east Texas saying goes, "It doesn't get much better than that."

As the reality began to sink in, I found myself walking around thinking, *Why me? What have I done to deserve such an award?*

If hard work qualifies someone, I'm no different from millions of Americans who get up and go to their jobs every day, pay their bills, and earn enough to provide their families with food, clothing, and shelter. But the awards ceremony was scheduled to take place on May 1, 1992, at the Grand Hyatt Hotel in Washington, D.C., so I didn't have very long to think about why I'd been chosen, or what I would talk about in the speech I'd have to make. I had given lots of speeches to school-age children, and I was fairly comfortable doing it, but this one was going to be in front of hundreds of very important people who had accomplished great things. "Wow," I said to myself. "I wonder if it's too late to back out."

At some point, everyone pauses to reflect on his or her own personal history, and I am no different. This was my time. One day, as the reality began sinking in, I grabbed a tape recorder and started looking for a place to be alone for a few moments. I went up to the corporate exercise room, where I never go, and took a seat on what is called an exercise bike. That didn't last long. Now I know why I don't go up there. It's like sitting on your thumb. What I need is a *tractor* seat. I got off it immediately and sat on the steps.

Here I was, chairman of the board of this company, seeking privacy in my own domain. How had it all happened? How did I get from there to here? Memories came flooding over me. I sat there for over an hour with the tape running, weeping uncontrollably and telling my story into that little machine. Afterward, I was totally drained, but I composed myself somewhat and went into the rest room and washed my face with cold water. I handed the tape to my liaison officer, Don Jacobs, and said, "I've been working on my speech for the Horatio Alger Awards. See what you think of this."

Don later called Melba, saying, "You have to hear this speech!"

"What did he say?" Melba wanted to know, and Don

detailed some of it to her. She later told me that she had wondered if I'd blurted out the whole story.

Melba came to the office to hear the tape, then she and Don confronted me and said, "It *is* time to tell the story."

In my own eyes, I was just a little, short, fat guy from Texas who sells tacos for a living. But others seemed to see something more in me. They called me a man who had risen all the way from nobody to somebody through hard work and dedication. Trying and failing, and trying again. Getting knocked down time and time again, but always getting up again, with constant reinforcement from Melba, believing in myself no matter what.

I was also painfully aware of what it cost to get here, and of my many failings as a human being. Such an award *causes* one to reflect on such things. I had been driven by fear and shame and anger to run away from my problems instead of turning to face them, obsessed with proving that I could make it. I guess I still felt deep inside that, with all my efforts to become a better person, I would never be able to absolve myself. If all these good people felt I was worthwhile after all, maybe I finally was beginning to grow into the kind of man I've worked so long and hard to become. In answer to Horatio Alger Association executive director Terry Giroux's question, Melba would later say the most important moment of her life was when I won this award because it gave me the "approval" I had been seeking all my life.

But I knew there was something more, something I still hadn't outgrown, something I'd never come to terms with, something I'd spent my whole life running away from, something deep inside that I had always been too ashamed to admit. I might not ever be truly free from the past, might never be the man I knew I could be, until I could admit it—and proclaim it for all to hear. If I could bring myself to confess that I spent most of my life as an illiterate, that I had become a multimillionaire and made a huge success in three straight business enterprises with varying degrees of reading deficiency, I might be able to inspire millions like myself, and those with even more crippling handicaps, to rise above their liabilities just as I have. Now, *that* would make me feel ten feet tall.

I knew that this declaration of independence from the past would have to begin with my own family. First and foremost, with my beloved Melba. So in our home one night, I took her hands in mine and told her with all my heart that I would spend the rest of my life, if necessary, making it up to her for all the pain I'd caused her because of the pain I was going through myself. We wept in each other's arms.

Melba saw the need to lay the groundwork so that if word leaked out that I had been illiterate, our sons would at least be aware of it. There was no way of knowing the results of this new focus on us. She didn't know it was going to keep getting bigger and bigger, but she did think it would be a good idea to let Tommy and Mark know.

On the other hand, I saw no reason at all to divulge something that was part of the past. As bad as it was, I thought it simply did not matter anymore. It was embarrassing enough to think about privately when the memory occurred to me, and I sure didn't want it out in the open. In fact, I thought of canceling the meeting with the two boys.

Probably, neither would be able to believe what I had to say anyway—that I had never learned how to read or write in school, that illiteracy had put a chip on my shoulder, forced me to work harder than other people just to keep up with them, had cut me off from my family and from everyone else but Melba, the only one who knew my secret. They would think I was just making excuses for not being there for them as children.

I know I do things differently, and knowing myself better than anyone else, I think I have figured out why. Older readers will know what I mean when I say I grew up in a time when you had to be tough. I went through a lot as a youngster, and my attitudes were formed around these experiences. I couldn't prevent that any more than I could prevent my becoming ill with polio. And at the same time I don't apologize for it. I can't. I believe, for better or worse, I am what God made me.

So after much thought, we called our two sons, Tom Jr. and Mark, now grown and married with their own families, to join us in the conference room of our company headquarters the next week.

Flashbacks? You bet! They came in *droves* prior to that meeting, like flying calendar pages in those old movies signifying the passage of time. Most of my recurring thoughts centered on *work*. As a man who always believed in working eighteen hours a day, seven days a week, in order to get ahead financially and provide for his family, I admit to being absent many times when I probably should have been there for my sons, and for Melba too.

I wasn't there when they needed me. I was out selling vacuum cleaners, and later recreational vehicles, on the road constantly, and it always seemed that when some birthday or other big deal for them came up, I was forced to make a choice—be there or be out trying to make a living. If the boys were doing something like earning another feather in the Indian Guides, or hoping against hope their daddy would be home for their next Boy Scout event, I usually was earning another dollar in some state or other to make sure they always had enough to eat. They needed me there at their functions, but I needed to pay the bills. It was like being a member of the Rotary Club and never wanting to miss a meeting, but then, just before noon, an important call comes in and you have to take it. It was never about golf or anything like that.

I feel that I provided a good life for our sons otherwise, and if I'm to blame for anything, then so be it. I've always done the best I could do at the time, and admittedly, the extended absences went on throughout their childhood. Perhaps some readers will understand.

I was thinking all these things prior to that fateful December 10, 1991, the day Melba had called the meeting. And I knew that our sons, now mature young men, were still feeling the sting of my absences. They couldn't help it. I was hoping somehow this confession would draw us closer, was hoping it wasn't too late for us to become the loving American family I'd always wanted. Not Super-family, just *typical*. How wonderful that would be.

Miss Melba had wanted the meeting, saying we could maybe start with a clean slate, so I said, heck, let's give it a try. It got off to a bad start. Immediately. They thought something had to be wrong. Usually when they were called for a meeting in the *boardroom*, it spelled trouble with a capital T, and I admit that usually was the case. I'm the characteristic CEO father, and they're their father's sons. This is America. Let freedom ring, and let the people work.

The meeting had been set for one o'clock on a Tuesday afternoon, and they didn't come in smiling. It was foreboding. Melba assured them the world was not coming to an end or anything like that. Absolutely nothing bad.

I told the receptionist at the front desk that the only telephone call I'd accept would be from God, and we all filed into the corporate boardroom. Melba closed the blinds facing the busy hallway outside, and we took our seats, the boys on one side, and Melba and I on the other. For equality's sake, I purposely avoided sitting at the head of the table in my usual chairman's position. Then—surrounded by walls decorated with large framed photos of the dozen or so popular and successful restaurants Melba and I, along with Victor Gonzalez, had built, worked in, managed, and maintained—two people who knew poverty and illiteracy firsthand prepared to try to explain it to two well-fed, educated sons who stood six-foot-four and six-foot-three, respectively.

"Your dad wants to bring you up to date on some of his background," Melba said in answer to their quizzical looks.

I've got plenty of rough edges, and I couldn't keep thoughts from surfacing as we settled in to talk. And I confess, I suppressed a few old and not-so-old resentments. Any honest father in the United States will agree with me. But, as I have grown older, I guess I've mellowed somewhat about a lot of things, one of them being the totally different outlooks on life my sons and I have. I've been slow to accept the realization that every generation is extremely different. Mine was different from my dad's and my sons' are different from mine. Having grown up hearing of the horrors of the Great Depression, you learn what it's like to do without and to appreciate any and all of the good things that come your way. That, coupled with the adversities I had faced over the years, made me work twice as hard for everything.

This was the area in which we had had most of our disagreements. My sons have never really known adversity. Therefore, I have not been able to instill in them the same sense of urgency that drives me. In their own ways, they have paid their dues, I suppose, but my work habits are such that it is very difficult for me to understand why everybody else isn't the same. In fact, I just don't understand it at all, and that's the way it is, so help me Walter Cronkite.

So there we were, eyeball-to-eyeball, when Miss Melba took the lead.

"We have something very important to tell you, and maybe it will help you to understand why your dad is the way he is sometimes," she said. "He didn't want to do this, but I urged him to, and he has agreed."

We were all very nervous, and I was probably highest on the stress scale. I was about to divulge a deep secret only Melba and I had shared. *Why do it?* I thought. I had succeeded in life in many ways, had dealt with high-powered boards of directors, attorneys, bankers, CPAs, actuaries, and the like, and yet here I was about to let a different cat out of the bag.

"OK, guys, here goes," I said, getting the ball rolling. I told them about being a sick kid. They had known some things, but not much. Not all the painful aspects of my illnesses, not the whole story of my total lack of education, not the less-than-perfect life I had lived, and certainly not the most dreadful part of all—my illiteracy.

This was one of the most difficult things I'd ever done. Was it emotional? To say the least. Especially when I choked up while relating to them the fact I'd always been a slow learner in school, unable to catch up with kids younger than I was, and becoming so frustrated I just doodled and daydreamed and never paid attention. I told them how I fell into that habit, even when attending Sunday school and church with my dad. The department leaders or preacher would make announcements of upcoming events, and I simply didn't listen. I figured someone would pick up on it and at the right time let me know where to go or what to do. To an extent, I'm still that way today. I don't back down from anything, but just like a bloodhound, sometimes I have to be pointed in the right direction. Once I get the scent, look out, here I come.

Then I explained why I had been tough on them about homework, and extra book work even when they were in bed sick. If they weren't on the verge of dying, I made them study the lives of U.S. presidents, things like that. I didn't want them to lose interest for an instant and lapse into what I had suffered through by being unable to read and write. In my own way, I guess I was looking out for them, even if they resented me for it at the time. I confess, I'm heartless when it comes to work. Work is the American way, and it's Tom Harken's way. Someone told me this is the twentieth century . . . Sometimes I think I'm still living in the nineteenth. It better describes my attitude about work, and yes, I have put those boys through their paces with backbreaking toil. I wanted it to toughen them, teach them, *reach* them. But God help me, I never wished illiteracy on them. No one should have to suffer that.

Tempers flared a time or two, but as we continued talking, they began to realize why their mother had swooped them out of my lap as kids when they clambered up wanting me to read the Sunday funnies. I just couldn't do it. And they were finally coming around to understand why I'd always ordered cheeseburgers in restaurants. I couldn't read the menus, so I always played it safe.

My tone eased then, and I began telling them how it had hurt to be unable to help them with their homework when they needed assistance with their simple spelling words and things like that. That's when the room grew very quiet. Melba and I wept as we told it all, not holding anything back, supporting each other through this as best we could. The boys weren't fully comprehending it all yet, but it was sinking in. Their eyes grew moist, and their hearts seemed to soften toward me just a little.

"I remember some of it," said Tommy, the older of the two. "It's coming back to me now."

He recalled how Melba would grab him off my lap when he wanted me to read to him, telling him, "Your dad is busy, let me do it."

At about this point, Tommy got up and walked around the table and hugged me, saying, "Oh, Dad, I'm so sorry. I didn't know it then, but now I can understand."

Tears poured from our eyes. Mark was a bit reluctant, and I can't blame him. He was still remembering all those times when I wasn't there for him, and I know he deserves to be bitter about it. Like when he got the grand prize for his Wizard of Oz Scarecrow costume one Halloween, or the time he made a triple play in Little League—I wasn't there. He took it a little harder than Tommy did.

There were times when Melba wouldn't be in the room and

one of them would approach with a schoolbook and ask, "Dad, what's this word?"

I didn't *want* to be curt with them, didn't *mean* to be, but it always sounded like I was when I'd be forced to say, "Go away, son, I'm busy. Go ask your mother." That was tough to do, but that is what I did and what I felt I had to do back then—had to hide the fact I couldn't read, had to keep it buried, down deep where it hurt, and where it still hurts.

I can imagine how people with AIDS must feel. You tend to build a brick wall around yourself. Then at some point, if you decide to remove the wall and tear it down one brick at a time, ultimately you feel that you are all alone in this world. So it's natural to wonder how people are going to accept you once you divulge embarrassing secrets. This doesn't make it any easier.

Being unable to read words on a page didn't prevent me from being able to read between the lines, and it became a habit, then a talent I honed to perfection over the years—sizing up a situation. If I do say so myself, I can do it instantly and thoroughly, and I was definitely reading between the lines with our two sons in that conference room. If the younger son was a bit slow in warming up to me, which was one of the purposes of this meeting, I was trying very hard to reach Mark's heart. I maneuvered the conversation around to Melba and how she had struggled so hard to help me hide the secret and to always, always protect me, and that did it. Mark was moved.

We stood, all of us, Mark included, and we hugged, and we cried.

At that moment, my years of pent-up frustration eased, and relief surged through me like a fresh breeze. Melba seemed happier, too, and with the boys, it was the questions. Here they came: How could you be illiterate and be on a bank board? How could you negotiate land deals? Start up companies? Thoroughly understand complicated contracts? How could you drive a car all those years without a license, especially when you made us get our driver's licenses? That was almost a tough one to answer.

They wanted to know everything all at once, asking how I had run six retail travel trailer lots, how I became an independent distributor, selling in five states, overseeing managers, how I had handled all that paperwork.

"Dad, you owned a percentage of an auto agency, a trucking company, motorcycle business, Southland Distributing Company, Revedi, Inc., and now you own restaurants."

How? How? How did you do this? How did you do that? they asked, wanting to know everything. The questions were popping right and left, and I was giving back answers as fast as I could. For instance, in a big bank meeting, maybe I had "forgotten my glasses." Plus, I had to be the most alert person in any meeting or whatever. Melba says I seem to be able to hear at least two conversations at once. In sales, with a lot of information memorized, I would call Melba on the phone, and she would write up the orders. In advertising meetings, I came up with ideas and dictated policies, and no one ever questioned whether I had read over any existing materials. I just made it sound so good, they *assumed* I'd read it.

I also explained to Tommy and Mark that I'd always been good with numbers, so profit-and-loss statements, known as P&Ls, were no problem. Don't forget, either, that Melba was tutoring me throughout all that time and though I wasn't good with phonics, I was picking up words at a rapid pace by memory. So, I was quickly learning the words *overhead, profit,* and *loss.* Especially *profit.* That always jumped right off the page at me. No problem there. And I could catch a discrepancy quicker than a seasoned CPA.

Incidentally, it's one thing to learn a lot of words by recognition alone, but quite another to read them on a page with a lot of other ones that you don't recognize at all. And recognizing them was much easier than writing them, let alone trying to spell them, when you couldn't see them pictured in front of you.

Tom Jr.; his wife, Debra; and their children, Trace and Terran

Mark; his wife, Staci; and their daughter, McKenzie

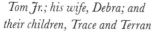

But the lesson I was trying to teach our sons was the fact that I never allowed myself to be trapped in a corner. Born with the love of freedom, I had to learn the trap-avoidance technique early, and it stayed with me—right up until today, even though I eventually learned to read. It requires more than alertness and nimble feet. It's an eternal vigil of the inner being, a subconscious mind-set with a built-in alarm, and when that alarm goes off, I go into action. I've relied on such instincts long enough to know it works, and a lot of my friends who head up huge corporations, universities, churches, government bodies, and the like, will agree. Someone has said you don't know your own strength without the struggle, and much of my struggle was in this realm. I came to know my own strength because of it, and I cultivated it to my own uses in order to get ahead in life. If avoiding traps, or even unpleasantness, is a downfall, so be it, but I believe it's a talent worth having.

Miss Melba picked up the conversational answers where I left off, and I really don't know how long that meeting with our sons lasted. It *seemed* like an eternity, and I do remember feeling totally drained but still not totally convinced that I'd done the right thing. Still, there was so much yet to be done—like hugging them more often from then on out, saying that I was proud of them and their accomplishments, and, yes, telling them that I loved them more than they ever could imagine. Our sons bade us loving good-byes and prepared to leave for their homes. We all embraced again, a family at last, with all the barriers removed. By this time, the office had closed for the day, and our employees were long gone. Miss Melba and I remained a while, quietly reflecting on what we'd done.

"It was something you needed to do, and you've done it," she said.

Maybe so, but at that moment I was wondering about what the boys would be saying about all this, and what's more, to whom. Melba says she didn't take my illiteracy as seriously as I did and she never thought any less of me because of it. In fact, as she puts it, I was so intelligent in spite of it, that she had enormous respect for me, as well as a great deal of compassion. But it still produces a queasy feeling in the pit of your stomach at all times and is a cause for concern, so I always take it seriously. I take everything seriously. That's the way it is when you come from hardworking German stock. And to be totally honest, at that particular moment, I was considering my feelings more than those of anyone else. It sounds selfish, I know, but it boils down to survival.

But Melba said it was the right thing to do, her thoughts somewhat calming my fears and soothing my feelings. It was time. And it was. Recently, I asked my boys how they felt about it all.

"We may have been uncomfortable now and then, but we never felt unloved or anything like that," Tommy said. "When you were growing up, your parents were always within arm's reach of you, so I think you must have developed a lot of guilt due to not being right there for us at all times."

"Thank goodness you weren't," Mark said. "Or we might not have survived."

Locking up the offices for the night, Melba and I walked out into the mid-winter evening and toward our separate cars, hand in hand, without saying a word. I think we were still a bit dazed with what we'd just done—telling our secret.

We arrived home a minute or so apart. Melba went into the kitchen to prepare some food, while I sat at my desk in the library-office, both of us busying ourselves, but strangely quiet. For the space of a half hour, she came in and kept returning every few minutes to say something like, "You did the right thing . . . It's going to be OK."

I knew she was thinking deeply about something, and finally she came out with it. "You have a speech coming up at the Rotary Club. You're a community leader who will be speaking to community leaders. You've always searched for your true purpose in life, and this may be it. With literacy being spoken of so often and so openly these days, maybe you should tell your story. Maybe it will help people, cause them to say, 'If he can do it, I can do it.' After all, it only takes a miracle."

And a miracle it took. When you're speaking to 350 powerful community leaders, it's a bit different from being in the boardroom with a wife and two sons. I felt awkward and my anxiety had to be obvious as I stumbled through my talk that day, but the audience was deeply understanding. The whole experience brought us closer to the community. Yet, these were my friends and neighbors; I was still uneasy about opening up to the world in Washington, because I planned to relate more of those small, touching details, like how I couldn't read to my sons. Things that few think of when considering illiteracy. But what I had revealed in that boardroom, and to the Rotary Club, helped tremendously a few weeks later when I disclosed our long-held secret to the Horatio Alger Association. I didn't know it at the time, but those were the first of almost six hundred speeches I would be giving over the next few years. Speeches on overcoming illiteracy and making something of one's life. It had started right there in that boardroom, where the silence became deafening after the words were uttered: "I was your father, and I couldn't read."

Washington, D.C. What a city! It was so impressive that everything in my past paled and shrank in comparison, including my newfound confidence about my former problem, the big *I*: illiteracy. When we arrived in the huge ballroom at the Grand Hyatt on the big evening, I was sure my speech was going to bomb and my palms began to sweat as three of us stood backstage awaiting our turn—Maya Angelou, James Rouse, and myself.

As the quiet, gentlemanly Rouse received his Horatio Alger Award and delivered his acceptance remarks, my throat went dry and my head began to spin. It really and truly did. As he finished, a hearty round of applause came from members of the association, all previous recipients, their guests, and the fifty-plus teenage winners of Horatio Alger scholarships. Then, as an introduction to my own speech, came an overly complimentary five-minute video documentary of my life, and it was my cue to push aside the curtain and walk to center stage.

One of my favorite emcees, along with Ed McMahon, Horatio Alger Association member Tom Haggai, nodded and stood to the side. Waiting, distinguished and erect and with a proud smile on his face, was W. W. Clements. Around my neck he placed a red ribbon holding a huge golden medallion imprinted with a likeness of Horatio Alger and signifying membership in that illustrious organization. Then he presented me with a bust of the man for whom the association is named, and the deed was done. I was a full-fledged member.

That was the easy part. Now I was expected to make my speech. At that moment, my throat felt swollen shut. Talk? I was doing well to breathe! But I had to do it. Foots was walking off, and Tom Haggai had retreated into the shadows. You could say the stage was mine—and I didn't want it.

Mentally grasping for something familiar, I put off the speech another millisecond by improvising a line:

"Thank you, Foots. Folks, for those of you who don't know, Foots Clements is better known as *Mr.* Dr Pepper! Thank you, Foots, very much."

Well, that got a nice round of friendly applause. Hey, maybe this wasn't going to be so bad after all, I thought. Swallowing hard, I grasped the edges of that podium so tightly that my knuckles turned white. Then I peered out into the semidarkness until I could see the adoring face of Miss Melba, the smiling faces of my family and all the friends who had come to be with us and share in our joy—including my old boss and his wife, Jim and Mable Lou Sperry—and plunged right in before I lost my nerve.

"I can't believe I'm really standing here," I began. "I'm just a guy who peddles tacos. But here I am on this stage beside these great Americans to receive the Horatio Alger Award.

"The Horatio Alger Award most definitely is the Oscar, the Emmy, and the Tony of *real life*, and I accept it on behalf of those hard workers everywhere who share an unstoppable dream.

"I thank the Horatio Alger Association, and I congratulate

the other recipients, along with this fine group of young people who are receiving scholarships.

"Also, I want to express appreciation to my friends who came from all over the country to spend a few moments with us on this great occasion.

"And to my family—sons Tommy and Mark, and their wives, and a fine grandson, Trace, who is two going on *twenty-two*.

"Behind every good man is a great woman, and I have the greatest woman in the world who walks beside me, and at the same time stands behind me all the way. My beautiful wife of thirty-three years—Miss Melba.

"As you have heard, I was ill with polio for years as a child. When I got back into school, I was a big kid at a little desk. And soon everyone realized that I couldn't read or write. I was illiterate—the 'dummy, dummy bell' who couldn't read or spell.

"That was tough. Times were tough. I didn't know what else to do—so I dropped out.

"Time went by, and I found myself selling vacuum cleaners door-to-door. Believe me, that's tough too.

"But I had no problem *selling* them. I just couldn't write up the orders. I had to train myself to remember names, addresses, account numbers—then when I got home, my wife would write in the details.

"Only Melba shared my embarrassing secret all those years. No one else knew what I went through, especially when our sons were small and wanted their daddy to read them bedtime stories.

"All I knew was *See Spot Run*, and let me tell you, Tom Harken felt like running too—right off the face of the earth.

"But we got through it, and on the tenth of December, I told my sons the story of my illiteracy, and how Melba taught me to read and write over the years. They had never known, and I believe it drew us closer together.

"Now, thanks to that great lady, I can take Trace upon my lap and read whatever he wants to hear. Yes! Yes! Yes! Yes, I can!

"My journey through life has not been an impossible one. For a while, it was just a little harder than most, and I feel I am the better for it.

"Exactly thirty years ago, as I walked those hot, dusty streets of Beaumont, Texas, knocking on a hundred doors a day *maybe* to sell one vacuum cleaner, I had a dream of becoming independent, free and clear. I had the American Dream.

"There was a light at the end of the tunnel, but let me tell you, it was a tiny speck of light for a long, long time.

"Slowly but gradually, it grew, until now. I've just exited the end of that tunnel into this room. And I never dreamed the fullness of that light would shine as brightly as it does—reflecting upon the eager young faces here who just can't wait to get on with life. I know that feeling. I still have it, and I say to you— *Keep* it. *That* is the secret.

"Each one of you has a tunnel to go through too. And you're just beginning your journey. But thanks to a little guy named Horatio Alger, and to great men like Dr. Norman Vincent Peale, Dr. Robert Schuller, and many others who were inspired by his success stories—thanks to the Horatio Alger Association, you won't have to enter that dark tunnel alone.

"You will take with you the *lamp of education*, and only you can decide how brightly it will burn. Pump it up! Light your way!

"The harder you work, the more fuel will be added. Go out and build taller buildings, higher bridges. Whatever your individual *vacuum cleaner* is—sell it, and become the best.

"Your families and friends must be very proud of you tonight. So am I, and I say go out there and conquer this world and help make it a better place to live.

"I expect to see better cars, I expect to see better airplanes. I expect to see better products of every description, I expect to see the environment cleaned up and turned around, and I expect that after ten, twenty, or thirty years, you will find yourselves here again, and you will have the opportunity to pass along the story to a younger generation of how you did it.

"I expect all this because I plan to stick around and be here when you return. By then, you will know what a joy and a privilege and an *honor* it is to pass along your experiences and encourage someone else. That is the *greatest* reward of all.

"Thank you, everyone, for this award. For this night.

"I will never forget it. My family will never forget it. God loves you, I love you, and God bless the United States of America again, and *again*, and *again*!"

As those final words rang throughout the ballroom, I watched in amazement as a thousand people rose as one to reward me with a standing ovation. Tears streamed down dozens of faces. Was I crying too? Or laughing? To this day, I don't know, but I gazed down at Miss Melba and the boys, their eyes locked with mine, and I knew this was the most moving moment of my life.

As I left the podium, Maya Angelou was waiting backstage to follow me with her own acceptance speech. The daughter of a sharecropper who had risen to become her country's poet laureate, she was, and still is, one of the most revered women in America. I was in awe of her, but when she looked at me, tears in her eyes, she opened her arms and grabbed me in a huge bear hug and lifted me right off the floor.

And that was just the beginning. At the end of the ceremonies, I was stunned to find a long line of dignitaries—including fellow Alger Award recipients—waiting to shake my hand. I felt like apologizing for making them wait to see me, but they didn't seem to mind. One of them was General Colin Powell. Another was Mary Kay Ash. Then the beloved entertainer and author, Art Linkletter. Even the ones who had just received the award with me, including former Secretary of State Henry Kissinger, a refugee from Nazi Germany who had not only carved out a life for himself in the United States but left his mark on the history of his time as a champion of democracy. Taking me aside a couple of years later, Dr. Kissinger would say, "Tom, out of the thousands of speeches I've heard in my lifetime—speeches made by presidents and kings—I remember only about five. Yours is one of the five I will remember."

I was thrilled, and a little intimidated, to meet General Colin Powell at the 1992 ceremony.

One of those who came up to congratulate me after my address was Dr. Robert Schuller. He walked up to me, placed his hands on my shoulder, and told me he wanted me to appear as his guest on the *Hour of Power*. As Miss Melba and I held hands that night on the way to our room, reliving all the memories, she said to me:

"Do you know what you agreed to tonight?"

"No, what?" I asked.

"You agreed to tell our story on Dr. Schuller's program with all those millions of people watching," she said.

"I did? Oh my gosh! What have I done?"

13

Selling Literacy

This is why I really learned to read—quality time with my grandkids.

❖❖❖❖❖❖❖❖❖❖❖❖❖❖❖❖❖❖❖❖❖❖❖❖

Television makes you look bigger than you really are, so I hoped I would have time to lose thirty or forty pounds before my guest appearance on the *Hour of Power* in late 1992. But in the following months, I think I *gained* thirty. One morning as I started getting ready to go to work, I happened to step onto the bathroom scale and suck in my stomach just as Melba walked in.

"That might help, honey, but how long can you hold it in like that?" she said with a smile.

"Hopefully long enough to be able to see the numbers," I

answered, determining to slim down before facing Dr. Schuller's immense congregation.

When the big day finally arrived—Sunday, November 1—I was all but a nervous wreck. Having assured the Schuller office there was no need to have anyone meet us, we'd flown into Garden Grove, California, and picked up a rental car the afternoon before. First, we drove to Dr. Schuller's church and walked the grounds, imagining a spirited young minister at the original site many years earlier, atop an abandoned concession stand ardently preaching to a collection of cars in an old drive-in movie theater.

Driving then to the Doubletree, we'd checked in, had a hasty dinner, and retired early. Prior to settling down for a fitful night, I had stood near the bed and carried on a hypothetical dialogue with Dr. Schuller while Melba listened attentively to some of the comments I planned to make on the air. Offering some thoughtful suggestions, she assured me everything would be fine. I dozed later, and my dreams were filled with the sounds of crashing glass as the entire church fell in when I entered.

Yet dawn found the edifice still standing and us hurrying to get ready in time for the car to be sent to pick us up for the short drive to 12141 Lewis Street, address of the famous Crystal Cathedral. While shaving and brushing, I was mentally rehearsing what I hoped to say. Along with nicking my neck, and tinting my tie with toothpaste, I could never seem to get past, "Good morning, Dr. Schuller."

Before I knew it, there I was, surrounded with potted palm trees on the dais of the cathedral. Along with the whole staff, Dr. Schuller and his gracious wife, Arvella, had done everything possible to make Miss Melba and me comfortable backstage before the ceremonies, but when the first of the three services finally began, my heart was pounding even with her there in the fifth row. I glanced out into the congregation of about twenty-five hundred or so, gazing at me from their seats, and made eye contact with her. There was that eternal spark of love in her eyes, that proud smile, and I knew she was thinking of what it had taken for both of us to get there, and what God had sent me to do.

At the same time, I was feeling a little like Moses at the burning bush. As I stood beside Dr. Schuller to begin our interview, all I could think about was the fact that somewhere between 22 and 35 million people were going to be watching me on television around the world, and my throat went as dry as the Gobi Desert.

"I'm a little nervous," I told him. "I don't do this every day."

"Well, Tom," he replied. "I don't do this every day either—just on Sundays."

That eased the strain. I could breathe again. We laughed, and I told our story. Both of us, and many in the congregation, were in tears by the time I told them about how it made me feel when I couldn't set my young sons in my lap and read to them. When I finished saying how grateful I was to Melba for teaching me to read and write, Dr. Schuller asked me how she'd found out about my illiteracy.

"She had to fill out the marriage license," I told him.

Dr. Schuller and I created a special bond that day as I spoke about our passionate commitment to the cause of literacy. It was a time when people were beginning to pay attention to the illiteracy problem, and he wanted to do what he could to help.

The videotape of that show was aired in early January 1993, and my life hasn't been the same since. The speech requests began flooding into my office, sometimes several per day. I was so delighted and exhilarated about the prospect of helping so many people that for the next year or so, I turned down very few requests. I'd drive to my destination if it wasn't far enough to fly commercially, and fly if it was too far to drive, all at my own expense.

It was an exhausting schedule, but I loved every minute of it and didn't regret a single appearance.

Melba says of that first year, "Tom had always been endowed—or cursed—with more energy than five ordinary men, but the Horatio Alger Award accelerated him into a perpetual-motion machine. Exploding with ideas and enthusiasm, he hit the ground running every morning, usually before dawn. He didn't stop until after midnight, and even then, he could hardly rest because of all the plans he was percolating for the next day. His life was a flurry of phone calls, meetings, and speech making. Always on the go, nonstop from one appearance to the next, he was a force of nature, believing absolutely in what he was doing and believing in himself. Even his wardrobe began to improve. I'd always had trouble getting him to put on a tie, and suddenly it seemed he was needing lots of suits. The gentleman in him began to come out. It was exciting just to be around him."

Out of more than six hundred scheduled speaking engagements, I missed only two, and these were during that busy year of 1993. On one occasion, I was ill with a high fever and totally unable to get out of bed. This was to be a speech to students at a local event, and my liaison officer substituted for me on that one. He'd heard our story so many times he knew it by heart. Sometime later, we were heading out to Bermuda to speak to a large group of business owners, and just before we boarded the plane, a relative of a dear friend caught up with us and said our friend had been killed in an accident. The family needed us, so we made a phone call, extended our apologies, and dealt as best we could with the tragedy.

During my speaking tours, with no book of my own to promote, I was often pictured holding aloft Dr. Schuller's latest volume, or *Parade* editor Walter Anderson's, or Tom Haggai's. Then, Chick-fil-A founder S. Truett Cathy presented me with his great autobiography, *It's Easier to Succeed Than to Fail,* and there I went again, helping promote another friend's book.

"What a title," I told him one day. "Wish I'd thought of it first."

"I've got a better one for you, Tom," he replied. "How about this—*Fake It 'Til You Make It.* After all, that's what you did, sitting on all those corporate boards and becoming a business success while pretending you could read and not being able to."

We almost used Truett's idea because, you know, he's right. That is what I did. It was a great idea—still is—but then an editor said it might encourage others to fake it too. Well, Truett didn't mean that, of course, and I most certainly wouldn't want to see *anybody* go through what I did. Heck, it's easier just to apply yourself and go ahead and learn to read than to go through the agony of illiteracy.

Soon I began going into prisons to speak to inmates, encouraging them not to take their educational programs for granted.

Some of these appearances placed me in perilous—at least very scary—situations. And for a guy who's still afraid of the dark, as well as his shadow, that can be serious. I can recall several times being shut away in a prison behind heavy steel doors with dozens of killers and some other bad dudes with what appeared to be very few guards. All I could see at times was one. But according to letters of thanks from prisoners and prison officials, the positive results of my talks far outweigh any thoughts of personal safety.

On one occasion at a prison, the inmates were shackled and the guards were alert and fully armed inside and outside a big room where a GED graduation was going to take place.

Once inside those walls, I was guarded closely and escorted everywhere I went. The graduates were over to my right as I approached the podium. The warden had introduced me, and under his breath he said, "Under no circumstances are you to hand over the microphone or get near one of these prisoners."

"No sir," I said, assuming he meant they were dangerous, and that one misguided yell over the public address system could incite a riot.

I told our story and congratulated the men, and then the ceremonies began with the presentation of awards and GED diplomas. This particular hard-core group would never be released from prison, but it was obvious they had a desire for a better life by being able to read about places they would never be able to visit.

During the question-and-answer session, one of the toughest-looking prisoners stood and asked if he could approach the podium. I glanced over at the warden, who shook his head no. I looked back at the young man. He had tears in his eyes but didn't care. He knew this probably was the last time he'd ever have any contact with the outside world.

"But Mr. Harken," he said, "I just want to say something to my grandfather."

Again, I looked at the warden. Again, he shook his head. But I turned back to the prisoner and said, "You bet! Come on over here."

"Thank you, Mr. Harken," he said upon reaching the podium. His hand shook as he reached out for the microphone, wiped his eyes, and cleared his throat.

"I want all of you to know that my grandfather is the old black gentleman over there wearing the old faded overalls. I'm sure he remembers back when I would make fun of him and his clothes," the young man spoke from his heart.

"Grandpa, I will never get out of here because I didn't do things the way you advised me to," he said. "But I got this GED because I wanted to show you I could do something right for a change. I love you, Grandpa. I'm sorry."

As his voice trailed off, in that instant, I looked over to the work-lined face of the old man in blue overalls, starched shirt, and scuffed work shoes. He had tears in his eyes, and it was obvious he'd never ventured far from his farm. But he'd come to this ceremony, and by golly, I was going to make it an even more special occasion for him, one he nor anyone else would ever forget.

I took the microphone back and told the grandfather to come up and give his grandson a big hug. The old man brushed a rough hand across his eyes, and with the boy's mother and sister looking on smilingly, he made his way, ever so carefully and slowly, to his grandson, hugging him, probably for the first and last time. Then, wondering how my brashness had affected the rest of the room, I looked to the warden, then to the guards. There wasn't a dry eye in the place.

Those are the kinds of moments that make speech making worthwhile—the grassroots efforts—but I also knew that literacy needed political help, so I became active in fund-raisers, backing politicians who were supporting literacy issues in Washington. Among them were a couple of good Texas friends, Senators Phil Gramm and Kay Bailey Hutchison.

This stumping for literacy has become my fourth successful career—after making it in the tough fields of vacuum cleaners, recreational vehicles, and the restaurant business—and it's proving to be the most exciting adventure of them all. I'm not making a dollar doing it—that's not what it's about, and there's nothing left for me to prove in that area—but I'm using the tough lessons I've learned about life to help transform other people's lives. At long last, it feels like the fulfillment of my destiny. After all the years I spent struggling to become a success, no matter what the cost, these are turning out to be the most rewarding years of my life, and Melba's.

In 1994 Miss Melba and I were honored to meet *Parade* editor Walter Anderson and his wife, Loretta. That was the year he became a recipient of the Horatio Alger Award, and we got to know them during the annual festivities in Washington. Walter is another dedicated advocate for the cause of literacy, and he was instrumental in my keynoting at the annual Literacy Volunteers of America conference in Buffalo that October. A dear friend of his is Ruth Colvin, founder of LVA, and apparently he had spoken to her about the little, short fat guy from Beaumont, Texas, who had a story to tell.

I will always remember telling it on this particular occasion. I had just finished my message, and it was time for questions and answers. In the audience, a very distinguished young black man stood, trembling and crying, and he couldn't seem to get out what he wanted to say. You could've heard a pin drop in that auditorium.

"Stay right there," I told him. "I'm coming to you." As I drew near, he became even more emotional. I knew he was in pain, and I knew what it was.

"Son," I said, "come with me."

Reluctantly, he accompanied me to the stage. Microphone in hand, I said, "Tell us what's wrong so that we can help you." By then, we were both in tears, and the audience, too, was crying.

"You know what, Mr. Harken?" he said. "Before hearing your story, I thought only black people couldn't read."

"I know, I know," I said, comforting him. "I'd always thought that *I* was the only person in the world who couldn't read."

We hugged, standing there for several moments with tears in our eyes. We were brothers—one black, one white—both with the same red blood. We felt it, and the audience did too. Today, that young man can read, and I only wish I could see him now. He has a whole new outlook on life because somebody cared enough to help him. As long as God is willing, I'm going to do whatever I can to open the doors for people who say, "Will you help me?"

That's why I give most of the people I meet a copy of *God's Minute*. Almost everybody needs one. People everywhere are in pain about something they think is beyond their control.

Something they can't let go of, something that won't go away, something that hurts so bad it's hard to think about anything else. It's a little verse that puts it all in perspective, that helps them through the tough times. It was given to me long ago by one of my mentors during an especially tough time of mine. Casey Southern said he'd been carrying it for years and it would help me. He removed the little frayed piece of paper from his wallet, handed it to me, and told me to read it, not knowing that I couldn't.

"Casey, it would mean more if you read it to me," I said to him. That was over thirty years ago, and I remember it so clearly. I wish I could give credit, but I don't think anyone knows who wrote it. It reads:

> I have only just a minute,
> Only sixty seconds in it,
> Forced upon me—can't refuse it,
> Didn't seek it, didn't choose it,
> But it's up to me to use it,
> I must suffer if I lose it,
> Give account if I abuse it,
> Just a tiny little minute . . .
> But eternity is in it.

God's Minute will comfort you through most anything. Come see me at a speech, and I'll give you a special copy for your wallet or purse. It's free—well, almost; if you want one, you have to give me a great big hug. You need that as much as you need the poem. So do I.

In speeches to retired people—teachers, businesspeople, laymen, it doesn't matter—I say, "Think of what you might do to help people learn to read. You have some unique talent that maybe only God knows about, but you can use it to help others. Someone nearby, or across the street or down the road, might consider it a *miracle* to be able to accomplish something you take for granted. Be observant, be aware. If you see someone falter in a certain way, you may recognize the fact that they're illiterate and need help. Or simply go offer your services at a library. I guarantee they'll be happy to see you, and you'll feel fulfilled again. Do it now. Get up off that chair and go do it."

It works. People are becoming volunteers all over the country. They're going into school systems and saying, "Hey, I read this story about Tom Harken and Miss Melba. What can I do to help?" They just need to be told they're *needed*. And to me it's really gratifying that more and more people are becoming tutors. And you know, it's the tutor who gets the most out of it. If you teach somebody to read a book—Wow! It opens up their entire life. Now they can be whole, now they can *be* somebody, now their dreams of what America is all about can become a reality, and *you* helped do it.

A perfect example of what I'm talking about was making a beeline toward me after one of my early speeches to a local literacy group. In the line of well-wishers waiting for a hug and a handshake, an elderly woman using a walker approached with a Bible under an arm and her tutor in tow.

"Mr. Tom, Mr. Tom," she said above the other voices. "You're not going nowhere until I get my hug, so you wait right there."

Well, that walker didn't slow her down a bit, and believe you me, I waited for that lady. She introduced herself, then told me that our stories were similar, and that she'd recently learned to read at the age of eighty-seven. In my speech, I had told about not being able to read to my sons while they were growing up, and she knew just what I was talking about.

"Mr. Tom, I couldn't read to my children, and I couldn't

read to my grandchildren, but now, thank God, I can read to my *great*-grandchildren."

"Wow," I exclaimed. "You're eighty-seven years old and you've just learned to read . . . That's remarkable. Can you read this?" I asked, pointing to the Bible.

"Yes, sir, I can," she said proudly.

"Of all the things to read, I've found that the Bible is one of the most difficult," I said. "Why'd you pick that book?"

"I'll tell you why," she said. "I've been a good woman all my life, and I always knew I'd go to heaven when I die . . . I just wanted to read the contract"

Bob Hope first won a Horatio Alger Award in 1968. Ruth Stafford Peale and I were glad to be a part of his receiving it a second time.

During my busy speaking schedule in 1995, I was helping plan a visit by Bob Hope for a first in the history of the Horatio Alger Association. I'd met Bob and his wife, Dolores, on several occasions. Back in the '80s, he was coming to town regularly to help raise money for one of his favorite projects, the Hughen School for children with disabilities, and he and Dolores would dine with us. I came up with the idea to make Bob the only person to ever receive the Horatio Alger Award twice. Originally he received it in 1968, and I thought he deserved to get it again.

In May 1996 I found myself back at the Crystal Cathedral for a second visit on the *Hour of Power*, and you'd think I'd have been over my stage fright by now. But I was beside myself once again as I waited for Dr. Schuller to introduce me. Since I refused to carry a script, as usual, Melba was crossing her fingers that I wouldn't say anything out of line, but there was no need to be concerned. This time, Dr. Schuller had a surprise for *me*.

A few months before, at the behest of literacy champion Walter Anderson, reporter Michael Ryan and a photographer from *Parade* had come to Beaumont to interview me for a story. I knew it was coming out, but just didn't know when—and I had no idea it would be a cover story. Dr. Schuller had a copy of it and showed it to everyone. There I was on the cover, reading to a group of kids, including my grandchildren. Me? Tom Harken? I was astounded, confounded, and dumbfounded, all rolled into one.

In fact, I was so overwhelmed at the experience of holding an actual copy of the printed story in my hands, it didn't occur to me until later, when Melba pointed it out, that I was appearing on the cover of a magazine with eighty million readers on a television program with millions of viewers worldwide. Now that will blow your mind!

That second appearance precipitated a fresh flood of speech requests from the largest to the smallest—hundreds of them—and once again I found myself unable to turn down more than a handful. I had enthusiasm to spare, and my motto was "Wake 'em up and shake 'em up." I wasn't a spring chicken anymore, and Melba was concerned about my trying to keep up with a schedule that kept me on the road and in the air most of the days of the month. But of course no one and nothing could hold me back, and I pressed on relentlessly through rain and snow, headache and stomachache, exhaustion and exasperation, from one end of the country to the other.

Me, Jerry Falwell, and Billy Graham
I present Dr. Graham, a 1965 recipient of the Horatio
Alger Award, with a copy of my book Quotations,
and another Alger book at commencement exercises at
Reverend Falwell's Liberty University in 1997.

❖❖❖❖❖❖❖❖❖❖❖❖❖❖❖❖❖❖❖❖❖❖❖❖❖

One September I racked up seven speeches in one day, flying by helicopter in nasty weather to different schools until they all looked the same. There were other appearances in Michigan, Washington, Oregon, and on to another national literacy conference in Tulsa, Oklahoma, where I renewed acquaintances with fellow literacy advocates Barbara Bush and then Miss America, Tara Holland.

I may stand in awe of the famous people I meet, but when it comes to meeting adversity head-on, a huge portion of my admiration and respect is reserved for many whose names may not be familiar. Names like all the great students in Virginia Clark's literacy class in Alhambre, California. After the *Parade* article came out, one of her students, Samuel Obara, wrote me a letter, and everyone in the class signed it, requesting that if I ever happened to be nearby, would I please come and say hello. Immediately, I decided to go. There was no way I could refuse such a wonderful group of immigrants who have come to the America they once heard about and now love. And did it surprise them! We enjoyed an evening of exchanging stories and hugs.

Promoting literacy keeps me busy, busy, busy.
(Captured by Terry Chaine in New Mexico, 6-26-98)

In the middle of 1997, the press began pursuing me like a political candidate. I'd always wanted to serve my country in some political capacity because I thought I had some good ideas and had a lot to offer in several areas. For several months, I had been getting calls from members of the Republican Party who urged me to run for the U.S. Congress as a candidate from my district.

Miss Melba thought it would be the wrong thing for me to do, but if I decided to go ahead and run, she was sure I'd win—and politics would never be the same again. Washington has a few so-called mavericks in town, she said, but nobody quite like Tom Harken, and she meant the Tom Harken from Texas, not the Tom Harkin from Iowa.

This editorial cartoon pokes fun at first-term U.S. Rep. Nick Lampson, who seems to breathe a sigh of relief at my announcement that I was not going to run against him. (Courtesy of the Beaumont Enterprise, *8-3-97)*

❖❖❖❖❖❖❖❖❖❖❖❖❖❖❖❖❖❖❖❖❖❖❖❖❖❖❖❖

Well, I gave a lot of thought to the prospect of running, but it didn't take long for me to realize I could accomplish my goals in life more effectively as a private citizen and businessman than I ever could as a politician beholden to all the special interests. So I called a press conference on July 29 to announce that I wasn't going to run for Congress, and that was the end of that.

It had been exhilarating for a while, but I was deeply relieved, and so was Melba.

My strong point, it seems, came from what once was my weakest point—illiteracy and the triumph over it, and if I could do it, *anyone* could—so I began to focus on even more speaking engagements. In 1994, I was honored to become a member of the National Advisory Board of the Literacy Volunteers of America. Wally Amos is national spokesman, so I suppose you might say I'm a mini-spokesman. I go where few others go. If a town's population is 173, then 174 of us show up for the speech. On an average, my audiences are comprised of from 250 to 500, and some range up to several thousand.

The preceding cases explain my reasons for doing what I do—the prisons, the little old ladies, the young people—but there are hard facts that accompany and round out each story.

The true purpose of this book can be found in both dry statistics and lifeblood experiences. I began promoting literacy in order to help a few people, but as time went on, some surprising truths were uncovered. I learned that forty to forty-five million people in this country cannot read, and that another fifty-plus million are functionally illiterate. That's a third of our country! No wonder our prisons are filling up faster than we can build them. This is a cry for help from those whose scars aren't visible but are there nonetheless.

At one point, the United States was tops in education. Gradually, we slipped, then went from fifth place to two hundred forty-seventh in the short span of ten years. According to recent information provided by the National Institute for Literacy, our functionally illiterate people continue to live in poverty, and the likelihood of being on welfare goes up as literacy levels go down. Three out of four food stamp recipients perform in the two lowest literacy levels.

Those at Level One display difficulty in using certain reading, writing, and computational skills considered necessary for functioning in everyday life. This includes barely being able to sign one's name, read a newspaper, or total a bank deposit. Adults at this level work an average of nineteen weeks per year, while those at Level Five work forty-four weeks per year. Seven in ten prisoners perform in the lowest two literacy levels.

I was fortunate enough to be featured in a recent issue of *Modern Maturity* in an article entitled "America's Dirty Little Secret," pertaining to illiteracy. In that article, Carolyn Staley, deputy director of the National Institute for Literacy, said, "Many people don't understand that literacy is more than reading and writing. It is the ability to access information, make decisions, and add to the overall quality of life." Truer words were never spoken, and we must double efforts to educate those millions who cannot read and write. All Americans can and should be doing more to address this country's literacy needs, says the National Institute for Literacy in revealing the sad truth that nationally, fewer than 10 percent of adults who *could* benefit from literacy programs are currently being served.

Part of the fault lies in the fact that we are shoving children through school in order to get federal money, and at the same time failing to do our jobs by seeing that kids are passed *with* an education, not without one. In Texas alone, according to state statistics, in 1997 forty thousand third graders failed a reading test and eighty-two thousand eighth graders failed reading, writing, or math tests. Yet nearly all of them were promoted to the next grade. Expand that to all fifty states and you can see that our educational system is contributing to the illiteracy of millions of kids a year. That has got to stop.

Some welcome news has come in the form of Texas governor George W. Bush's pronouncement that enough is enough. He has formed a plan to get extra help for students who cannot pass, calling for more than $200 million for such things as expanding reading academics and training teachers in phonics. Although Bush's plan is meeting with political opposition, ending automatic promotion has drawn strong support from education reformers, parents, teachers, and business groups. I believe the upcoming year will see a major difference in the way schools operate in Texas, thanks to Governor Bush and others who are vitally concerned with the future of this country and this country's most valuable asset: our children and our grandchildren.

But that is just in Texas. We must have tens of thousands more tutors all across the country, more people interested in helping others learn to read. This is a wrap, but it won't be a total wrap until everyone can read. Will you help me? (More information on how you can help will be found in the Postscript at the end of this book, including addresses, phone numbers and Internet web site locations.)

Some people dream of political careers, and some dream of fame, but the vast majority of us are happy if we can do something worthwhile in life, thereby earning and upholding a good name. My own dreams came close to dying an early death in Lakeview, Michigan, and my most vivid memories of growing up there are of pain and loneliness. For a long time, I've wanted to rid myself of those memories and make my peace at last with a childhood that has haunted me for so long.

So in late August of 1997, with the immediate purpose of helping with a fund-raiser for the Community Wellness Center in Lakeview, I took a sentimental journey home with Melba at my side. I'd returned a few times, but I sensed that for some reason this trip was going to be something special. That Saturday, the overcast sky cleared and a beautiful sunshiny day took over. As I was called on to make a few remarks to the crowd, I gazed out over their heads at the picturesque village where I grew up. So many things came back to me at that moment.

The road was dirt in those days, I told them, and I remembered the day it had been blacktopped for the first time. The lake had seemed much bigger then, and the movie theater is gone.

The older ones there that day knew my story of polio and then being shut away at home with tuberculosis. I told them about the frosty morning during this sad period when I was awakened by a noise outside my window. Rubbing the sleep from my eyes, I could see Dad beckoning to me. I made it to the window in time to wave good-bye as he left to open his grocery store. Then, I looked down, and in the snow he had tramped out the words, I LOVE YOU TOMMY. That was the last snow of the year, and I read those words every day until the spring thaw melted them away.

It was only after talking about such memories, fifty years later, that I realized my parents and I had shared a few wonderful experiences during a childhood that I had remembered only with bitterness.

During my long isolation in the bedroom, I had remembered only the meals that my mother left outside my door, afraid to touch me. But now I remembered all the times when I kept her company in the kitchen while she was cooking, and when I had helped her carry the food in a picnic basket to the home of a less fortunate neighbor.

I also remembered the anger and resentment I had felt toward my father for his kindness toward anyone and everyone in town who was suffering from illness or hardship. *Everyone but me*, I had thought at the time. But I had grown into the kind of man he was, and after all these years, my heart suddenly reached out to embrace him.

On that same trip, Melba and I visited the old house where I once lived. I opened the door to my old room—the one where Mom had left my meals—and I looked out the window into the yard of green grass. But all I could see was snow, where Dad had written I LOVE YOU TOMMY.

*My dad wrote I LOVE YOU TOMMY in the snow
outside my window in this house.*

We walked down the cellar steps where Dad had pretended to spank me for talking back to Mom. And I showed Melba the old furnace that I'd overloaded with coal one winter. There was much that was so familiar, and the place even smelled the same. But everything had mysteriously shrunk in the intervening years. Even the front porch where I'd learned to skate as a boy looked hardly bigger than my desk at the office today.

But after all these years, it had a warm glow that brought back my entire childhood, not the way I had remembered it, gloomy and joyless, but reimagined as a golden time through the eyes of a lifetime's experience. As we took one final look backward, standing there in the old house with the past pouring through me in a cleansing rain of memory, Melba and I held hands in silence.

My entire life had brought me on an epic journey—not of the trailblazing proportions of some great explorer or pioneer, but more like a map of where the life of a common man or woman might begin and where it can go. The journey had brought me full circle, and I had come home at last to make peace with myself. Melba stood beside me, as she has stood for forty years, and for the ten-thousandth time, I thanked God for bringing us together.

Epilogue

My favorite picture of my favorite person

❖❖❖❖❖❖❖❖❖❖❖❖❖❖❖❖❖❖❖❖❖

❧ By now it's probably clear to you that Tom and I have been an integral part of the other's life. We have been like salt and pepper or sugar and cream. Whatever we did, we did as a team. We started out as a team and grew as a team, always with optimism for the next phase of life. Not that we ever knew when or what the next phase would be, but whatever it was, we could do it *together*.

Certainly, in the early days of our life together, there were some very tough struggles. The toughest for Tom, of course, was the illiteracy problem. I don't think people can fully appreciate the severity of that problem unless they have experienced it or shared it with someone. Watching it gnaw away at his self-esteem was heartbreaking. Tom has always had the most positive and most upbeat attitude of anyone I've ever known. He has tons of common sense, which, from my point of view, is genius, and he's a person who makes things happen. As for problems, whatever I asked him, he had a clear solution. It might not always have been the one I was looking for, but it was always clear and made a lot of sense.

But when he was confronted with a situation in which not being able to read got in the way, it could really bring him down. His reaction was not usually one of dejection—although I knew it was there—but rather of frustration and underlying anger. And each time, all those problems had to be dealt with and tucked away because he had to go out the next day and face the world with confidence and a positive attitude. He couldn't let anyone sense his vulnerability. Those times were the toughest of all for me. Seeing the toll it took on him trying to cope with his problem was unbearable at times. But more than that, he had to keep the secret.

When Tom is talking to a group, he gives me far too much credit for his success. And certainly, I'm not so modest that I don't love every minute of it. But the truth is, we did it, as always, together.

Let me give you a little background from my perspective.

The first time I ever saw Tom, I thought he was a cute guy, but I was taken aback by his exuberance and enthusiasm. The second time I saw him, I thought, *Wow, this guy is for real!* It didn't take a rocket scientist to see that he had a lot going for him. I very quickly began to think he was the smartest guy I had ever met—*and* he was cute. So, when a few months into our relationship he informed me that he could not read, I truly was stunned.

What I came to realize later was that not being able to read does not mean that a person is not bright. It certainly was not true in Tom's case. He was far above average. He just didn't know it. And besides, he had lots of other positive attributes. He had motivation, energy, vision, and an unstoppable drive. Don't misunderstand me here. In my youthful inexperience, I did not know all these things then. However, I knew he could do anything, and I was going to help him. I knew that he would take care of the business end of things and I would take care of the nuts and bolts. It was as simple as that. Perhaps it was my upbringing that gave me stability and positiveness.

My Family

I grew up on a farm in Oklahoma—one of ten children, five girls and five boys. I was number eight. I was the youngest of the girls with two younger brothers. Mom and Dad were good parents—very solid, moral people. They had lived through and survived the awful depression. We were poor. I've heard a lot of people say, "We were poor, but we didn't know it." Well, we knew it! But we were not the only ones. Most everyone else in our part of Oklahoma was poor. Over the years I've taken a lot of good-natured teasing about being from Oklahoma. Most people tend to picture Oklahoma as this huge dust bowl like what they saw in the movie *Grapes of Wrath*. Well, we did have our share of dust storms, and we knew what to expect when the sky in the west turned brown. But Oklahoma is a lot more than that. It's a beautiful place, whose inhabitants are some of the best people you'll ever meet. They are genuinely warm, caring, and neighborly.

All of my brothers and sisters graduated from the same small country school called Consolidated Eight—Con. 8 for short—except for the two youngest. They finished at Roosevelt after Con. 8 closed for good in 1957. All twelve grades existed in one large building. At least it seemed large to me at the time. We had good teachers, some of whom were also local farmers, and they expected a lot from us. Apparently they were pretty great, because all of my siblings have been relatively successful with their lives. I have some wonderful memories of that little school where everyone knew everyone else. If anyone got out of line, everybody knew it. So you didn't want to do anything bad because everybody would know it.

There is certainly a lot to be said for the values you learn growing up on a farm in a small community like I did. You don't realize or appreciate those values until much later. At the time, all you know is that it is an awful lot of hard, hard work. This included rising early, milking the cows, feeding the animals, and working in the fields. When I refer to working in the fields, it sounds innocuous. But hoeing cotton in Oklahoma in the summertime is not as easy as it sounds. Scooping wheat and oats from the bed of an old truck under a hot, burning sun with the chaff going down the back of your neck is not fun either. But the real test is pulling cotton in August when the temperature is over a hundred degrees or in December with a blue norther blowing in and the thermometer drops below freezing.

Therefore, anything you could do to escape these things, you did. In our family, it was sports and doing well in school. Excelling in those two areas, along with knowing how to work hard, makes for a solid foundation. Also, there's nothing quite so creative as being poor.

A Difficult Story

The writing of this book has perhaps been harder on Tom than it has on his family. Several times, I urged him to give it up, just go on with life, and forget the past, but he couldn't do it. Our story had to be told, he said, in order to help others to seek help. This is true, and it has become something of a self-imposed duty. But also, I believe it had to be told to help him at last see that the little guy who always thought he was wrong has turned out to be right.

Due to his guilt-ridden illiteracy, Tom remembers the "bad" things, and there were many. But his loving family chooses to recall the good times. And in reality, Tom wasn't the ogre he thinks he was. Tough? Yes. Mean? No.

A product of his time, and of his unfortunate circumstances, Tom is a classic case history of the one twentieth-century generation that experienced a rigorous past and grew up into a more indulgent future. To a degree, so did I, as his wife, but perhaps this book will finally set the record straight. If hateful words have been spoken in the past, they are overshadowed by the love our sons and I feel for my husband and their father. He is a man, a provider, and a dad, and this is our love letter to him.

He always *wanted* to do the right thing, even when he couldn't, and we never held it against him because deep down, we knew.

True love helps make many things possible, but it must be combined with unswerving determination and a good measure of true grit. I was no pioneer woman of the past century—although I came from that stock—nor was I a superwoman of the future. But I *was* a girl of the '50s, a product of my generation, too, and once we met and I fell for him, I truly loved Tom. We wanted a home and a family, we wanted our future to unfold together, and I was willing to work hard to achieve those goals.

One example I always followed was that of my great mom, who toiled ceaselessly to make a life for ten children and a husband—my father—who was anything but easy. My mother's days were filled with drudgery, yet, she was brave, solid, resolute, and she provided the loving stability it always takes to keep a family together. I wanted a better life, and I wanted it to be with Tom, and the example of loyalty she set was the only one I knew to follow.

Tom sometimes describes me in such a way that you must be thinking that no one is *that* good! And you're right. I'm an ordinary woman, mother, and wife, just like millions of other women. I just happened to meet and fall in love with an extraordinary guy with a very unique problem. And I guess we conquered that problem in a kind of unique way.

Did I ever get discouraged and sink to the depths of despair? Of course—many times. I've cried a thousand tears—that's our release. But something deep inside me always pulled me back up, and I would move forward again. There are far too many great things to do than to cave in to self-pity.

I believe my childhood, fraught with hard work and deprivation, helped prepare me for those first years as Tom's wife. But so did the emotional strength most women inherit from somewhere. Outwardly, we can be soft and fluffy and overly sensitive, but when we have to, we can call upon that deeper layer of steel called inner strength and move mountains or have babies—alone if necessary.

When our first son, Tommy, was born, it would have been nice to know Tom was pacing the floor outside the delivery room—and for all I knew at the time, he was. In the 1950s, expectant fathers customarily were relegated to waiting rooms and expected to do no more than hand out cigars after the joyous occasion had occurred. My part in all this, no matter who was present, would be having the baby, and boy, was I about to do that! But through the pangs and pain, I looked forward to it because it was our baby. Tom's and mine, so in a way he *was* there with me, and the family I'd dreamed of was beginning.

Tom is as emotionally transparent as the windshield on one of his cars, so I always was attuned to his feelings and understood his frustrations. Even after becoming aware of the fact he wasn't "just outside the door" when our sons were born, I could feel the emotional trauma he'd experienced. It was his *reaction* to those frustrations that bothered me most. To me, it was *inaction*, and this I did not—could not—understand.

With ten dollars in his wallet, Tom was the perfect husband and father. "Bring home some milk? Bread? Sure, hon. Need anything else?"

But when, for some reason or another he was down to thirty-five cents and pocket lint, Tom became reckless and rash. When someone said desperate men do desperate things, the philosopher must have had Tom in mind because he became Mr. Desperation when he didn't have any money in his pocket. I didn't know this, and reacted accordingly, not by ranting at him but by being hurt. Then he would see that hurt in me, and it made him hurt even more. It was a vicious circle.

I had been raised in a family where we considered ourselves lucky to have meat on the table instead of our usual fare of beans and corn bread. Tom, who had grown up poor but in a mom-and-pop grocery environment, somehow thought food simply *appeared*. It took a long time for him to associate the amount of money we had at our disposal with the amount of groceries we could have in the refrigerator.

Of course, I was young and inexperienced too. Our sons never went hungry, but one night when the milk level was low and the bread was more than a day old, I said to Tom in exasperation, "Do you think food grows on trees?"

He must have thought it was a trick question. He considered for a moment, then said seriously, "A lot of it does."

Then, what I'd said struck me, and I collapsed in laughter. There were many times like that, just Tom and me, two naive kids, sharing life, sharing the hardships, and the fun. We could be driving down the street, and he'd say something, just make one of those comments of his out of the clear, blue sky, and we would laugh and laugh. During those hand-to-mouth days, it never occurred to me to give up. Divorce? No way. Murder? Hmm.

I had vowed to stay with my husband no matter what, and I intended to do so. He may have had a few faults (so did I), although for the life of me I can't think of what they may have been . . .

We were young, and Tom could be thoughtless at times. He

could make me the maddest! Especially when he would say something that really hurt. Going out the door in the morning, for example, he might say his piece, which was totally wrong, I knew—even if he didn't. I would stew all day, rehearsing all the things I was going to say to him when he returned and planning to really blast him. I even enjoyed rolling these things over and over in my mind all day long, just waiting for him to get back.

Then, when he walked through the door with a big smile and said "Hi, babe. How ya doin'?" in that way of his, my mind would go blank. *That*, of course, would irritate me even more—for my missed opportunity—but at the same time, my heart always went out to him.

Tom worked hard every day. That's one thing about him—he has always been a hard worker, and being something of a workaholic myself, this made me appreciate him all the more. I wasn't with him on his daily rounds, but when he would get home, I could see the tiredness in his eyes. Oh, I could become disgusted with the situation, but never with him. He *meant* well, and he was strong, *we* were strong, and optimistic. Even during the dark days, and darker nights, we always bounced back with our youthful enthusiasm and our love for each other. That's what kept us going when we had nothing else.

As mentioned, work was a common bond too. We sure weren't strangers to that. In the past, I had dragged sacks filled with a hundred pounds of cotton, and now Tom was knocking on that many doors per day to pay the bills.

Tom was such that he could make his illiteracy seem almost insignificant. Oh, it was hardly trivial to him, but he had that way about him that just made me forget he couldn't read nor write. Even when teaching him to read what, to me, were simple words, I never found myself thinking of him as being inferior in any way.

Everything else Tom did, his whole demeanor, overshadowed the fact he was illiterate. He was a unique and very complex individual, still is. He can be a man of steel, and a teddy bear. I believe part of the reason for this is that in his daily life he is constantly bombarded by mental images of when he *was* illiterate, and sometimes the old defense mechanism kicks in, washing away the softness and revealing a harder person, personally or businesswise. Being there at his side, I can attest to you that it was very, very painful. But I have also watched him overcome the impossible and reach new heights he never dreamed of. For that I am overwhelmingly and shamelessly proud.

It's been a whole new education just trying to figure him out. Any insecurity or frustration Tom ever exhibited was because of himself, or toward himself, and it was always short-lived. It didn't remain with him, it couldn't. After all, he had to go out and face the world again the next day. He learned early on to laugh at himself, and humor has played a role in the chemical magic we know. Even today, we can be driving along familiar streets, and Tom will be reminded of some foolish thing he did in the past. He will tell me about it, and we'll absolutely go into hysterics right there in the car.

Yes, at times, I felt overwhelmed, but what mother doesn't? Sometimes it seemed I was mother to three, referee, cook, and chauffeur combined. Everyone always needed something, or to be somewhere. All mothers and wives can identify with this, and those who survive take one day at a time. My faith—in God, in Tom, and in myself—never wavered, and that lone little hopeful dream, the one that had begun in rural Oklahoma, never died.

Postscript

There are many worthwhile organizations designed to help illiterate and functionally illiterate individuals. Below is a listing of the national headquarters offices of three such entities. Help is available. Pass it on. The magic words are,

"Will you help me?"

For more information on literacy, write:

The Literacy Volunteers of America, Inc.
635 James Street
Syracuse, NY 13203
315-472-0001
web site: www.literacyvolunteers.org

Laubach Literacy
1320 Jamesville Avenue
Syracuse, NY 13210
888-528-2224
web site: www.famlit.org

National Center for Family Literacy
825 Main Street, Suite 200
Louisville, KY 40202-4251
502-584-1133
web site: www.famlit.org.

For information on making educational endowments:

The Horatio Alger Association
99 Canal Center Plaza
Alexandria, VA 33214
web site: www.horatioalger.com

I have also put together a book titled *Quotations: Success Secrets of Power Thinkers* to commemorate the fiftieth anniversary of the Horatio Alger Association. It is available through the association.

A portion of the profits from this book will go to the Literacy Volunteers of America and to the Horatio Alger Association.